The Royal
African War Elephant
Restoring the missing piece of African History

Preface

The first of its kind, this commemorative focus is specifically on **The Royal African War Elephant** in history. This book's first and second editions are set to be distinct from any other history book in using war elephants. This book is a compilation of descriptions and illustrations of African War Elephants and their use in labor and war, depicted by cartographers and travelogues in rarely circulated images. It is considered a hidden history, now brought back into circulation for educational discussion and inspiration.

"The Royal African War Elephant" boasts a narrative that reveals hidden agendas and conspired motives and appreciates and magnifies gratitude for the travelogues, historians, and photographers of the Middle Ages. It lays out the institutional and cultural solutions paving the way for the future, restoring the kingdoms of African peoples. Images and depictions of the Royal African War Elephants throughout the ages are brought to their rightful place.

Learn about **The Kingdoms, The People,** and the quietly kept secrets of **The African Elephant** that played a pivotal role in world history.

Published by Media Management And Publishing LLC

Table of Contents

Athores Notes

Marquett J. Ivy extends his respect to esteemed scholars, historians, and enthusiasts of historical knowledge for their unwavering dedication to studying and preserving history. Their contributions have enriched our understanding of human history and illuminated the past.

From a background deeply rooted in African heritage, Marquett has been profoundly influenced by his upbringing. Born in St. Louis, Missouri and growing up in an environment that valued history, culture, and spirituality has shaped his perspective on life and the world. Holding the principles that this existence is God's being, where living beings inhabit God, and God inhabits them, making Him their habitation.

Marquett's educational journey began with a strong foundation in monotheism, instilling in him a sense of oneness with the divine. He pursued his education in institutions that emphasized African

American culture and history, further fueling his passion for understanding their shared heritage.

Throughout his formative years, he encountered challenges that deepened his appreciation for history, identity, and the legacy of his ancestors. This unwavering commitment to these ideals has been a guiding force in his life.

Having experienced life's highs and lows, celebrated achievements, and faced hardships, Marquett has gained valuable life lessons and shaped his

character. He has also been privileged to witness life's beautiful moments and mourn its losses.

We were embarking on journeys across continents, experiencing the rich diversity of our world, broadening his perspective, and allowing him to forge connections with people from diverse backgrounds.

For more than two decades, Marquett has embraced the roles of husband and father, instilling values of honor and resilience in his family, receiving letters of recommendation, and being awarded Illinois H.S. Association Father of the Year 2009, among various other organization certificates of appreciation. Additionally, he has served as a mentor, extending his influence to impact his community positively.

Driven by an insatiable curiosity and a deep passion for history, he delved into African history, explored the Moorish legacy, and studied Hebrew chronicles. This quest for knowledge has reinforced his belief in the interconnectedness of human existence and fueled his passion for literature and personal growth.

Venturing into music production and songwriting, Marquett has created compositions that inspire faith and reflection. These musical endeavors have ignited a newfound passion for the written word.

Marquett's forthcoming literary journey represents the culmination of diverse experiences, all guided by a profound sense of purpose. He hopes his work will inspire and educate, transcending religious perspectives to encapsulate the complex history of human systems and behaviors.

This journey is not merely physical; it is a pilgrimage of the soul, bringing the eternal essence of existence closer. In every step, every word, and every heartbeat, Marquette is reminded of the boundless grace that underpins his life's journey. He places the life principles and sacrifice of Yeshua Ibn Elohim at the forefront of his focus.

At the core of it all, the eternal spirit serves as Marquett's guiding light, infusing his work with a timeless message. He is dedicated to rekindling the spirits of generations, reviving heritage, culture, and spiritual essence. Marquett's literary endeavors seek to contribute to an understanding of humanity's intricate identities.

As people write and rewrite the narrative of their lives, Marquett's literary work, "The Royal African War Elephant," represents unity in diversity, all to the glory of the divine in our one human story.

Acknowledgment of Cited Sources:

Prelude

*A*s we chronicle the somber sagas of human strife and the stark inequalities that have been etched upon our past, we face an unerring truth - a truth steeped in suffering and agony. Within the fabric of conflict, a toll is taken, measured not in coin but in the precious essence of existence - the blood of the blameless, the wisdom of the elders, and even the unborn's potential. Amidst this desolation, a different facet emerges, glistening with radiant hope. A tale of fortitude unfurls, revealing the majestic bravery of those who withstand the tempests and rise above the ashes of adversity.

But as the banner of victory is unfurled, shadows cast a pall, shrouding the jubilation. The triumphant echoes of one civilization, tribe, and nation resonate, rippling through the scrolls of history. Yet this triumphant march often carries within it the specter of devastation, the chains of subjugation, and the tendrils of deprivation for other people. Amidst the crucible of African history, the intricacies intertwine, unveiling the stark dichotomy of our journey. From the birth pains of nations and peoples emerges a symphony - a symphony composed of strife and sacrifice, courage and valor, and lives surrendered and lost. Here, amidst the crucible of trials, courage and mettle, weave a splendid tableau, a testament to the undying strength of the human soul.

And as we reflect upon the battles waged by the old empires across the expanse of Africa - the North, the South, the West, and the East - their tales reverberate within these chronicles. In unity, we listen

to the cry that echoes through time, the cry of all descendants of Mother Africa - those who have been lost to history, to the ravages of war, to the scourge of enslavement, or the dominion of empires. We stand as one, connected by blood, shared family history, and unyielding determination. We pay homage to the valiant warriors and peoples of the continent - those who fought for self-determination and spiritual enlightenment, seeking the recognition and right to eternal life and generational freedom.

Critical thought and critical thinking about history and African history precisely. Especially regarding military, literary, building, and masonry, key points of value. The ancestral, national identities that foster pride and resilience should be understood that in processes of war and subjugation, these would be key points to be subject to destruction first. And the implementations of systemic institutions of suppression embedded deep in the foundations of societal structure.

It should be crucially noted at the outset of studies into African history and of the accounts of travelers and observers that the absence of documentation and observations of people's interactions with the elephant on the continent of Africa should in itself. I suspect there is inadequate documentation simply because of human nature and curiosity, as well as the fear of these animals that draws people from around the world just to see the animal with their own eyes. How people interact with it, and the absence of these early documentations is proof of omissions, but we will deal

with this later in this endeavor. So, let us move forward in this wondrous adventure.

My journey begins with unicorns: unicorns in the Bible. Within the language of the scriptures, the image projected with a unicorn is a horse with a horn in the center of its head. Mythical in abilities and beauty but also adorned for battle in war armor in the Old English depictions. Reading the Bible and understanding the stories of history with such a profound point of reality of people and places. I began to see that something was wrong, something is wrong with the Bible because out of all the stories of Egypt, Africa, and Ethiopia, the oxen, the horse, the bear, the lion, and the Leviathan, the great whales and crocodiles are the only animals mentioned. This negates the reality of the royal African elephant and the rhinoceros, the signature projections of power and dominance on earth. In understanding the course and stages of the creation of the English Bible and even the Bible as a whole, specifically with the English translations, atrocities, and abuses documented extensively to the destruction and exclusion of books and the blotting out of words. All passages for the use of enslavement and books were omitted. To not imprint images or ideas of revenge, retributions, or demands for restorations and repayments for wrongdoing and abuses that spark a fight for freedom beginning in the soul by the breath of God. It took place in different parts of the British Empire. The destruction of the Bible and its configuration varied from region to region depending on the government's empowerment of the people in subjection and enslaved to labor and rape. It is also why miseducation and the banning and refusal of education for the

enslaved, specifically in the reading of literature, was implemented. I hesitate to say that refusing to educate or banning reading, at least, shows reverence not to distort what is considered to be The inspired word of god, to be better than downright altering the book,? I will clearly say not so. Injustice is all the same. Additionally, within that is also why dehumanization was necessary, to deem one, not even a part of world history in itself, to indicate everything in these texts has no relation to the enslaved, which is quite the contrary in the most absolute.

The variations from the North American and Central American regions of the Caribbeans and other areas of the British Empire survive and are still preserved. The enslaved American Bible is one notable preservation. The Slave Bible was titled Parts of the Holy Bible and selected for the use of the Negro Slaves in the British West-India Islands.

It's not hard to understand, but it's only understood once you know why and then you see it. Understanding that the common sense of history is missing from documentation and illustrations for the same reasons that are public results of war and destruction and obliteration of people, I'm missing from history to destroy people's ability to resist force. And the first place of resistance is that of the mind. As the actual battlefield, once force has been able to get a foothold, the battlefield of the mind is easiest to maintain through disassociation of authority and responsibility. If the people have no right to a land, they have no reason to fight for a land.

If the people have no history to defend, the people have no destiny to implement empowerment of sovereignty.

As sovereignty begins in the mind, it starts with the conscious thought of why. Concerning the elephant, in African history, it is the power and majesty of the elephant, the rhino, the giraffe, and the lion that are the first associations we have with Africa. And for all the scholars and travelers of history and illustrations of kingdoms that authors and scholars have taken pen to paper to journal, there should be endless stories and illustrations of these animals in society, customs of culture and ceremony, and war. Butt when you raise the common sense of the matter and the stories of folklore, the first argument of descent to the glory of the continent is. "We don't have a lot of evidence". "There's very little documentation". "What sources do you have to back that up?" The answer is that war is in the mind first. And the first things to be surrendered in war are weapons of war. Fleets of ships have been destroyed, and as a result of defeat, weapons, armor, and defenses have been gathered together and destroyed. Also, as a result of defeat, entire artworks, history, embodiments of identity, power, and war have been destroyed. It should go without saying for those who are in the know and those who have studied actual history and documents. They know that these things are suppressed and why. It is the responsibility of those for whom this information is not only empowering but also part of their identity. They are all responsible for maintaining and preserving these facts, and this responsibility has fallen upon them. Miraculously, it is in the hands of us all. It is

our shared history of the world, our family, our honor, our glory, and our diversity of kinship. It has been established that some institutions and artifacts should be off-limits in times of war and must be protected at all costs.

The most powerful historical validated text of African history or in this one book Evliya Çelebi travels. "Ottoman Explorations of the Nile: " 1685 before the time of Napoleon. Evliya Çelebi, A Ottoman Turkish delegate commissioned trained and sent to explore The Nile River. Fully documenting the travels the peoples with the details unrestricted. The graphics circumstances of the ancient world and of the African history in its raw form within the book is utterly mind-blowing and was only in the Turkish language for many years and even after translations it is never quoted in regards to African history. But now available in the English translations. As it is clear, as we discussed earlier that cartographers map makers and envoys served multiple purposes for empires mapping out rival territories in the form of envoys bearing gifts and trade. But the details in this history or undoubtedly the most valiant of horrors as well as first hand experiences in the turbulent years of sub-Saharan history field with triumph as well as defeats. But the focus of this work is the restoration of Sub-Saharan history to English speakers and seekers. the quotes throughout this book will be centered in the Kingdom of Funj the modern territory of Sudan. For the sole purpose of the connecting of Nubia, Kush, Ethiopian Abyssinia as the founding lineages of the connective African civilizations. Gaining a proper understanding of why these histories were Blacked are multifaceted. As a proud African and lover of human

history to know the chronicles of the kings of the origins of mankind and the dramas of time on the African continent is unbound wealth. The stories and histories of the kings and kingdoms that we are responsible to tell and maintain is a honor beyond comprehension. The second edition of this book will contain chronicles of stories and dramas of the chronicles of kings and families and the histories of our humanity to forever be remembered and studied like no other land.

To us who are responsible for the memory, commemoration, admiration, respect, honor and expansion of the future of African history, this work is created. The compilation of this work is to me again a source and inspiration to the memory and recital of oral histories concerning the cultural perspective of pride and honor. It is to us who choose responsibility and for us benefit through African and world history to bear the responsibility. Projecting these histories and identities into the future. It is without doubt quite possible that technological advancements that as we know, could lead to the very destruction of society and civilization and dispersal of access to information globally. Therefore, it is paramount that remembrance of traditions and methods be maintained as a default mechanism that embodies the companionship of man and beast as the foundations of civilization and to ensure a swift response to navigate possible calamities or near extinction. The deeds and exploits of means and methods that undergird the foundational principles of societal structure between animal and human life must be preserved in mind, and the cultures, blood, and languages must

never be forgotten. And to swiftly identify any approach or attempt to diminish or impede pride, the cultures, and the identity of our African history.

The subject of this work is that of ancient culture, history, and civilization up to the present. Although the challenges of Africa and the future of Africa and African people are valid topics of discussion, they are not addressed without first addressing restoration and respect for those things diminished. Africa's technological, political, and physical scientific advancements are in the hands of those fields and professions and of the business and working-class support for these mechanisms of interlocking institutions that determine African people's protections, privileges, and rights according to the nations. This book is a unifying tool of sources to keep, maintain, and preserve some traditional folklore, mythical, traditional, and historical events put together as a body of work in its editions for the community and personal library of Depictions, descriptions, and traditions of the Royal African War Elephant.

These illustrations depicting Africans riding on African elephants in a military formation in cultural headdresses and apparel representing the People of the location in an organized defensive force exist as fact and have lived for over 400 years as a fact. Relative to the illustrations of hieroglyphs and artifacts of ancient civilizations and cultures related to the same migrations of people, it is irrefutable and, by definition, prehistoric. There would be no record of who or from where the first mount was recorded.

Logically, seeing that all these things were already taking place before Herodotus... Let me say again that it is worthy to note, and I repeat, that these illustrations depict Africans riding on African elephants in military formation, and cultural headdresses and weapons representing the people of the location in organized defensive forces exist as fact.

Within the course of this work, not only are the citations and illustrations from European cartographers and explorers, but we have also chosen to identify the traditions and documentation of the people by their accounts. Not in a capacity to disassociate but to reassociate African history with African scholarship, folklore, cultural traditions, and ceremonies. The main reason is that it would be inappropriate to dictate a foreigner's history of their land on association or irrespective of their scholarship. The etymology of the word scholar is scholaris in Latin Old English scolere "student, one who receives instruction in a school, one who learns from a teacher," from Medieval Latin scholaris, "a pupil, scholar," noun use of Late Latin scholaris "of a school," from Latin schola. There was a difference between a scholar and a scribe. The meaning of the word scribe is to write or to write down. To which scholarship is not document-related. The scholarship is to teach and to be taught.

One might even say that scholarship is being taught how to teach. Nature is the first teacher, one's father, mother, and community. And it is that community to which one is accountable for the provision and survival of life and development of values and foresight of being. What is written has a value to last, and then do

the ages as we have seen the ancestria writings written in stone, but confidence in documentation is also equally damaging through the intent of deception. The book of 1 Maccabees 3:38 read, "And laid open the book of the law, wherein the heathen had sought to paint the likeness of their images."

At this juncture, let me again disclose and provide this disclaimer to the respect and honor of the cultures and the heritage of the many people of the continent. Concerning the vast oral traditions and histories of nations in their ancestral structures. It should understand that the people themselves define terms, honors, and dishonors. It would also be understood that while one custom country or people might find offensive, another would not. Origin of War is the violation of territory, breach of personal rights forced captive servitude, and dehumanization.

One of the most significant complications, misunderstandings, and offenses with religion and five religions is an attempt to formulate an agreement of speech with the same language, definitions, and terminologies of sound, which means that, unless you say exactly what I say in response to what I believe and what you believe, we are not the same, unless you reply with the nearest same reply to my question. As an answer, we do not believe the same. If what you believe is defined differently in a different context of words, we will not be the same, and if we do not believe the same, one of us is wrong. Although this is not a religious body of work, it is a body of historical deceptions, narratives, and war-related communications. Not in the sense of implying a militant mindset or disgruntled

perspective. This body of work is solely to identify areas of history purposefully removed, covered downtrodden, demonized, and downplayed cultural histories and artistic representations to be of little to no value, which is the psychology of the battlefield of the mind.

It would seem like nothing to say that these representations are just stones, it seemed like nothing to say that these images that cartographers illustrated on the map are believed, it would seem like nothing to say that just because there are mythical stories and folklore and cited oral histories of battles and triumphant tales of Kings in their genius and organization, the peoples and cultures related to these histories should find little value, but I say to the contrary. However, these images are old, and stories renowned and aged of time and wisdom in a previous era of humanity, the very revival and maintenance of traditions teach a lesson all to themselves. It is a lesson for all people and cultures of ancestry. It is this: if a people lose control of the burial grounds of their fathers and mothers, a stranger to the land will dig them up, claim them as their own, and make their descendants pay to see their forefathers, especially if these kings were the foundational kings of civilization. It is easy to tell a people's relative culture to land by how they respect the dead of the land, being one with the land and forefathers.

The maps created in the centuries, the inquisitions, and the enslavement plan of the global religious forces remove African people from the land of their ancestry, disconnecting the pride and

sovereignty in following the instructions of their forefathers, which is the very essence of identity. In the Hebrew scriptures, the things that Moses presents to the great pharaoh of Egypt the foundations of what nations are made of most miraculously. We see the Bible translate the making of a people as a free people. If you are removed from your land, you cannot sustain yourself; if you remove Identity, you cannot define yourself; and the last is to remove the ability to defend yourself. We will touch on this later in many aspects.

Identify, define, and defend yourself. Identity is pride, and a restoration of pride is a restoration of identity that can only be maintained by the defense of the mind first in this present time. We are responsible for our protection, stories, culture, traditions, values, and identity. And we are responsible for our future.

Introduction

For the sake of our children, for the freedom of the mind, for the generations to come, and the ancestors of our fathers and mothers who bore us, of those who have fallen, and those who have risen in the glory of life, freedom and divine rite with authority, in the Eternal Spirit of the Living Breathing Salvation, I am writing this Book. It is the result of having been trained by teachers well-versed in the identities and histories of the world's people. The human family is one, and we all share history. However, it may be distinct portions attributed to specific lineages of inheritance, bestowed on some by no means of their own, but it is our history, our story. A history not bound by region or competence, status or dominance. It is existing divine providence that all that is not erased exists to multiply. These stories, histories, heritages, cultures, and triumphs to survive, thrive and multiply are with us today by no mistake.

This book is to be a work of compilation throughout the time given to me to document my travels and discoveries in better establishing an order of the facts to amend additions of information, sources, documentation, and verifications throughout the continent and honorably place the peoples, cultures, and proverbs of the civilization cultivated by African peoples relative to the companionship between God, Man and Beast in ceremony Life, Labor and War.

In an era characterized by immense uncertainty and unprecedented technological advancements, including artificial intelligence and the reshaping of human existence at its core, the significance of cultural heritage and historical remembrance reaches its pinnacle. The world finds itself amidst a transformative period, with Africa, its continent, nations, people, families, and diaspora holding the key to shaping the future of the global economy and determining the world's destiny. While acknowledging the contributions of other regions, Africa stands apart as a continent that draws claim from every ancestral human, unrivaled by any different landmass. This assertion may be subject to debate, but in recent history, there has been a surge in recognizing African people as the originators of the human race, the mythical garden of Eden, and the cradle of civilization.

It is crucial to approach these statements with caution, scrutinizing them for potential hidden agendas, repatriation motives, or fraudulent intentions, as no other people rooted in Africa can make comparable claims elsewhere in the world. Understanding this disparity highlights Africans' inherent disadvantage, both on their continent and abroad. When seeking accuracy, respect, and a deep appreciation for history and culture, it becomes essential to differentiate between factual, actual, and historical perspectives. Historical debates, archaeological dating, and documentation are multifaceted fields influenced by global politics, racial undertones, and economic considerations. The use of sources, dates, and numbers can be approximated and subjected to debate. Therefore, it is advisable to refrain from fixating on specific details that can give

rise to doubts, as information providers' credibility, honesty, and integrity may be called into question, potentially leading to legal and financial ramifications. This is an inherent characteristic of institutional formations, which aim to control and regulate the flow of information to maintain social order and structure.

The sources of information I will present in this discussion are likely to be considered questionable and secondary, subject to debate and scrutiny. Such narratives often face skepticism due to the dominance of foreign-sponsored literature, scholars, documents, and educational systems. To gain a broader understanding, it is recommended to seek original, unedited manuscripts dating from the 1884 Berlin conference to the pre-colonial century and explore research conducted in the native languages and scripts in which some manuscripts are written. However, this endeavor often leads to limited access and edited versions of content online, necessitating direct communication with individuals who possess knowledge of the scholars or authors of these works and are fluent in the respective languages or scripts. Even then, it is important to recognize that human politics have historically influenced scholarly works, mainly when kingdoms or rulers employed scholars to create narratives justifying wars, enslavement, land acquisitions, and other self-serving interests.

This indispensable tome is an invaluable addition to any personal library. With profound reverence for the majesty of nature and the Eternal Spirit of Creation, let us journey back to the ancient civilizations and heed their wisdom. It is a universally

acknowledged truth that humanity has learned invaluable lessons from observing the intricate behaviors of animals. Indeed, animals have been our greatest teachers, surpassing any knowledge we have imparted.Consider the extraordinary interplay between human ingenuity and our exploration of the natural world, guided by the innate intelligence of the creatures that inhabit it. The elephant, renowned as the pinnacle of earthly existence, possesses a profound intellect and understanding. Its comprehension of humanity extends beyond mere recognition; elephants possess a remarkable ability to interpret our communications, even following the direction indicated by a pointed finger. It is not that we have tamed the elephant, but rather that we, as the last emissaries of creation, have discovered life's principles with the animal's intricate social structures and hierarchies.One might surmise that the audacious notion of riding an elephant would never have entered the human mind had we not observed birds perched upon their mighty backs or witnessed primates deftly traversing the terrain astride these noble creatures. In unfamiliar vegetative landscapes, we can discern the poisonous from the nourishing by observing which foods animals choose to consume and which they leave untouched upon the branches. So, as this literary marvel takes root in the fertile soil of knowledge entwined with common sense and documented history, let us embark upon a transformative journey. Let the pages of this book unfurl before us, illuminating our minds and inspiring us to explore the paths of wisdom.

"Once you carry your water, you will remember every drop."
~ African proverb

"Interior Africa"

Map: 'Africa Interior.' (Interior Africa / Central Africa with Ethiopia, Oman, Libya etc.) With decorative cartouches showing Africans, elephants, crocodiles, lions, etc. Original copperplate engraving on verge-type hand-laid paper.Description: This authentic print originates from: 'Notitia orbis antiqui, sive geographia plenior by Christoph Cellarius, ed. published in Leipzig by Johann Frederick Gleditsch in 1731-32. Ref. Brunet I, 1724. Ebert 3868. An early standard work on the geography of Classical Antiquity was first published in 1686. Artists and Engravers: Author: Christoph Cellarius (1638 - 1707) or Christopher Keller was a German scholar, historian, and textbook publisher. Cellarius held academic positions in both Weimar and Halle. Cellarius's most important work was his 1683 publication, 'A Universal History Divided into an Ancient, Medieval, and New Period. 'This work introduced the concept of history as divisible into three distinct periods (Ancient History, Mediaeval History, and Modern History). It impacts the way future historians would interpret the past.

Chapter 1
Axum

(African Proverb)

~When the elephant falls, even the ants will kick him~

"Abraha, an Ethiopian Axumite Ruler, invaded Arabia with an Army of Royal African War Elephants in Golden African Armor, 70,000 men, and 150 maritime ships."

Ethiopia, the land of God. Ethiopia, land of the Kings. Ethiopia, the Land of the Blacks (Kush Khem). We must begin with this understanding. Let me repeat: We must understand that there is no one narrative. History is a puzzle piece put together by the narrative of many nations with individual interests and agendas; each narrative plays a role in a nation's history and the history of self-identified nations and self-defined nations. They are the center of the universe.

Visual attributes do not distinguish identity but by the name of Fathers and Mothers in the narratives of self-identified nations or sayings of divine purpose and living existence. From the empires of Ethiopia, we will begin with Axum. When trying to encapsulate the understanding of an empire regardless of the region of the world, one must take into account the vast ethnicities that make up a region, a kingdom, and an empire, and these plights and issues among the peoples and generations of distinct ancestries, have narratives themselves, of victories and losses, abuses as well as triumphs, as these are the attributes that

create identities, and cultures of people, binding them together. With respect to each empire we highlight in this book, there is also the remembrance of those lost families, destroyed lineages, and lives silenced by history. This first narrative is the perspective of the ancient Greeks and their documents on the glory, beauty, and majesty of African people, namely Ethiopia, Beginning with Evliya Çelebi travels. "Ottoman Explorations of the Nile:, Al-Hasan Ibn Muhammad and to Herodotus.

Now to Axum... where we begin to unravel omitted histories and questioned narratives by first securing that which is protected writings. Which are paramount for modern history and civilizations across the continent of Africa. But before we do this, let's break down the Kingdoms and people.

Here are the respected clans, Nations, peoples, and identities from ancient to modern. The mixture of Kushitic, Shemitic, and Khemitic in the region of the Axumite Empire during the time of Abraha: To whom we will mention in the next segment.

Aksumtes
Oromo
Beja
Nubians
Himyarites
Sabaean
Blemmyes
Meroites
Hadramawt
Tigrayans
Amhara
Agaw
Tigre
Gurage
Afar
Somali
Beta Irael

The Axumite Empire stood in an innumerable mixture of people's West, Central and most Southern regions of Africa during that time.

Ethiopia's regnal lists consist of recorded catalogs of monarchs who, according to tradition, held the country's throne. These lists are documented in manuscripts or transmitted orally through the generations by monasteries.

"Ethiopia mountain fortress Magdala"
1800s

Many extant regnal lists, both in written form and oral transmission, trace the lineage of rulers, commencing from Menelik I down through the Solomonic dynasty. According to Ethiopian lore, Menelik is reputed to be the offspring of Queen Makeda (the Queen of Sheba in the Bible) and King Solomon. Successive to Menelik, the royal lineage encompassed rulers from the Axumite, Zagwe, and Solomonic dynasties. Additional rulers who reigned before Menelik are cataloged in disparate Ethiopian narratives. These regnal records served the dual purpose of substantiating the enduring reign of the Ethiopian monarchy and furnishing legitimacy to the Solomonic dynasty.

"An alternate Ethiopian tradition asserts that the roots of the Ethiopian monarchy trace back to Khem, who was the son of the Biblical prophet Noah. While Khem's name isn't featured in the previously mentioned Biblical regnal list, a claimed genealogy that connects Khem to the founders of Axum does exist. According to this particular tradition, the establishment of Axum occurred

within a century after the Great Flood. This genealogy documents a line of kings descending from Khem, associated with Ethiopia and Axum. E. A. Wallis Budge called this lineage the 'Dynasty of Kush.'

Enno Littmann documented a tradition from an Ethiopian priest named Gabra Wahad, who recounted the following genealogy: Khem fathered Kush, and from Kush came Aethiopis, after whom the country was named Aethiopia. Aethiopis was interred in Aksum, and his tomb remains known today. It was believed that a perpetual fire was used to burn within it, consuming any donkey excrement or other materials that fell into it. Aethiopis begot 'Aksumawi, 'Aksumawi begot Malayka 'Aksum, who also begot Sum, Nafas, Bagi'o, Kuduki, 'Akhoro, and Fasheba. These six sons of 'Aksumawi played the role of progenitors for Aksum. When they decided to apportion their land, a man named May Bih arrived and, as the story goes, divided their land as an intermediary. Each of the six granted him two acres of land, and he settled among them.

Exert
"Mounting The Funj War Elephant"
Expedition
-Evliya Çelebi Travels
1685
"At the time of the morning prayer the trumpets and drums and kettledrums sounded Y399b and the march began.

Now Husayn Oan summoned this humble one and offered to take me up on his Mahmudi elephant, where he was already mounted. "By God." said 1. 'this is the first time I have ridden an elephant,' He let down a ladder woven of elephant skin. Reciting the Mu awwizatayn (the final two surahs of the Qur an), I clam-bered up to the kiosk on the hack of the elephant and settled in knee to knee with Husayn Qan, and then we set out. The King of Berberi was also with us, as was the dabir of Funjistan indeed, he had invited 13 men to join him on the elephant's back, and we sat there clustered together, cating our breakfast

34

and cutting stages (1.0., travelling fast). But this elephant moved in such stately fashion that the tea and fennel in our cups did not spill one drop, although a thousand elephants and even horses could not keep up with him. After breakfast, other elephants came abreast with ours. They had mounted on them the firdilans; that is, the singers and musicians. They played a kind of square rebub (rebec) and another instrument consisting of 200 iron rings attached to a hoop and making the sound kivi kivi, and there were also reed instruments accompanying the songs sung in a fine and melancholy voice hy the Funji singer. So we rolled up stations (i.c., travelled apace) enjoying these "Bayqara' musical sessions."

BABY RHINOCEROS SHOWING FIGHT IN CAMP

"In Darkest Africa"
1890
Exert
Evliya Çelebi
Another Berberi tribe hunts giraffes and elephants and rhinoceroses and gazelles in the deserts and cats these animals on the grounds that they have cloven hooves. [...] In fact, the servants of our host caught a baby giraffe and made kebabs from its flesh, It was incredibly fat. They offered me some and I ate it, God willing, it is permissible (helal); I have not seen anything about it in the legal texts. [Description of the giraffe)

35

Y405a [...] Because of the mild climate there are lovely boys and girls. The boys have doe eyes and dark skin and red faces, and an elegant manner of walking and talking. They are truly the progeny of the Prophet Noah. But they hardly wear any clothes: they only wrap themselves in a Berberi ihram (see note at Y311a) and a Berberi loincloth. They plait their hair. They are skin and bones, and sunburnt as though they have heen fried in hellfire. But they are very courageous.

Exert
Al-Hasan Ibn Muhammad Ibn Ahmad al-Wazzan (Descriptions of Africa)
P.258

"An elephant is a wild animal, but it can learn. It is found in abundance in the forests."
"Ethiopia, there is another method of elephant hunting that I do not remember,"

"Although the elephant is a great and ferocious animal, Ethiopian hunters hunt many of it in the following way: They go to the dense forests, where they know that these animals rest at night, so they set up there among the trees strong crossbars that form a thick fence, and leave a small empty place there. Then, they attach a door to it and leave it flat on the ground as a perforated door that can be lifted with the closing rope passed quickly. If the elephant enters the fence after it sleeps (and wakes up), they pull the rope with force, and it falls into the prison; then, the hunters descend into the trees and kill the elephant with arrows, then take its tusks to sell them. But if the elephant came out of the enclosure, it killed all the people found.

"Ethiopian Highlands to the fortress of Magdala"

Description Landscape with Khoikhoi hunting elephants, Jan Caspar Philips, 1727

MANIER OM GROOTE DIEREN TE VANGEN.

Der Hottentotten manier om wilde dieren te vangen (The Hottentotten way to catch wild animals).
Peter Kolbe (1675-1726)

This lengthy passage illustrates the advanced tactics that demonstrated the craftiness of African civilizations even in ancient times. During my studies, I've delved into the writings of ancient Greek historians and their perspectives on Ethiopia.

Through their accounts, it becomes evident that the Ethiopians captured the imagination of these scholars. For instance, Herodotus's literary work "Histories" is often referred to as "The Histories." Herodotus discusses various cultures, regions, and events in this extensive work, including mentions of Ethiopia. "The Histories" is divided into nine books, each focusing on different themes and topics, portraying the Ethiopians as remarkable figures, extolling their exceptional height and beauty. In his narratives, he expressed how these individuals were regarded as the tallest and most handsome among all humans. This distinct characteristic, along with their lengthy lifespans, marked the Ethiopians as a noteworthy people of the ancient world.

Herodotus's insights into the Egyptian perception of antiquity provided an intriguing layer to my historical exploration. He recorded the Egyptian belief that both the Ethiopians and the Colchians were among the earliest and most ancient groups of people. This viewpoint shared with me through my studies, hints at the Ethiopians potentially being considered the original inhabitants of the Earth, as per this ancient Egyptian perspective.

Another ancient historian, Diodorus Siculus, also contributed to the tapestry of historical understanding. His writings unveiled a fascination with the land of Ethiopia. He spoke of the Ethiopians residing in a remote corner of the world, far removed from the conflicts that plagued other regions. Their purported longevity and robust health painted a vivid picture of a people separated from the troubles of war and strife.

Further enhancing my comprehension of ancient mindsets, Diodorus Siculus vividly described the Ethiopians. These accounts mentioned the presence of deserts inhabited by unique and monstrous creatures. Additionally, the Ethiopians' democratic form of governance, their excellence in stature and

strength, and their role as the pioneers of astronomy collectively contribute to the multifaceted narrative that characterizes the ancient perspective on Ethiopia.

While Herodotus and Diodorus Siculus presented these narratives, it's important to approach their writings with a nuanced understanding. These perspectives reflect the observations and beliefs of their times, offering a glimpse into the historical context in which they were formulated. Through my exploration of these historical texts, I've discerned a fascinating interplay of perceptions, beliefs, and accounts, all contributing to understanding African history and the storied presence of the war elephant prehistorically.

Africa 1st century
"Pygmies hunting crocodiles and elephants"from Pompei, 1st century (fresco)

This print presents the ancient fresco titled "Pygmies hunting crocodiles and elephants" from Pompei, dating back to the 1st century AD. is housed in the

Museo Archeologico Nazionale in Naples, Campania, Italy. Discovered within Pompeii's ruins, the fresco depicts a scene of adventure and skill, capturing the essence of African culture. The pygmies are portrayed as skilled hunters facing off against formidable opponents – crocodiles and elephants. This portrayal offers insight into native African populations and their interactions with the Roman Empire. The artist's attention to detail is evident in every brushstroke, bringing life to each character and animal on this ancient wall painting. Vibrant colors create a sense of movement and excitement, transporting viewers back in time. Preserved for centuries under volcanic ash from Mount Vesuvius' eruption in 79 AD, this piece provides a glimpse into daily life in ancient Rome. Its historical significance cannot be overstated, shedding light on cultural exchanges between civilizations. Bridgeman Images.

Here are some of Diodorus Siculus's quotes from a work titled "Library of History" ("Bibliotheca Historica" in Greek). Here are a few quotes from Diodorus Siculus that mentioned Ethiopia:

"Ethiopia, the most remote of all inhabited lands, is separated into two parts by the Nile River, each of which is quite unlike the other in its characteristics."

"In the region of the Eastern Ethiopians, there are vast deserts inhabited by four-footed beasts of monstrous shape, which are bred nowhere else."

"The Ethiopians have both a democratic form of government and a king, who is chosen for his virtue and righteousness."

"The Ethiopians are the largest and most just of all nations."

"Among the Ethiopians, kingship is transferred not from father to son, but from brother to brother, or from uncle to nephew, with the

eldest being the heir."

"The Ethiopians are said to be the inventors of the science of astronomy."

"In the territory of the Western Ethiopians, there are great and marvelous rivers which have crocodiles of enormous size."

"The Ethiopians have a wonderful breed of cattle, some of which have only one horn, situated on the middle of their foreheads."

"The Ethiopian kings are well known for their longevity, often living to be more than a hundred years old."

"The Ethiopians have a belief that the gods participate in human affairs, and they often send down prophecies to the kings in their dreams."

These quotes are translations and as such, language, ideas, and understanding is lost in translations. Sometimes, intentionally omitting certain words and unconnected verbal expressions defining experiences can cause complete misinterpretation. As in many languages, one word encapsulates an entire concept. As well as some words encapsulating complete ideas, numbers, and animals.

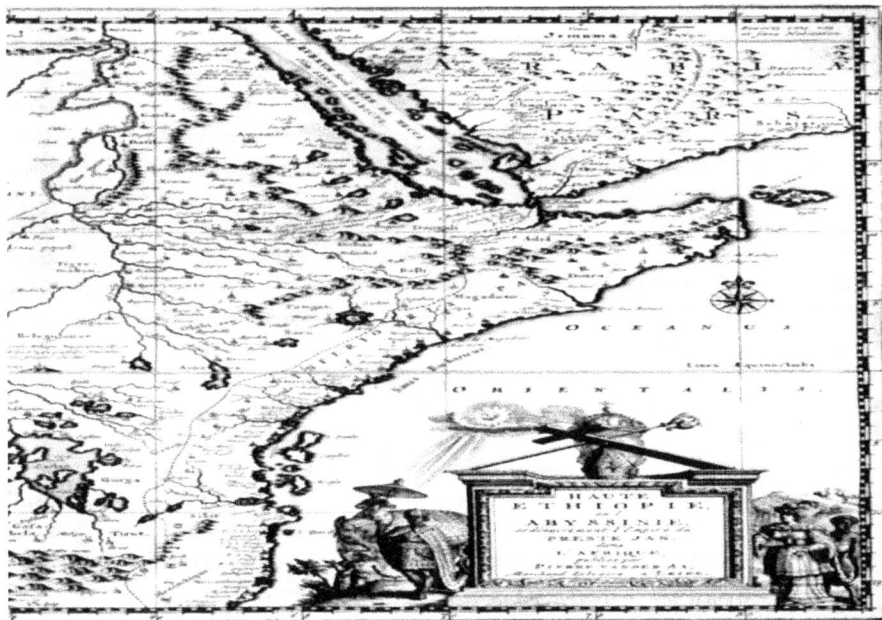

Central Africa, by Pieter van der Aa. 1713
Haute Ethiopie, ou l' Abyssinie, ordinairement l'Empire du Preste Jan, dans l'Afrique.
"Notice the emperor with mounted elephant escort.

Because of the reality of history and empire and the back and forth of regional territories and kingdoms overlapping takes us to the time of Negus "Kings" የንጉሶች ንጉስ yenigusochi nigusi.

The official languages of the Axumite kingdom (1st-8th centuries AD) in Ethiopia, Ge'ez (official), Sabaean, Greek, and local languages like Afar, Oromo, and Tigrinya Ge'ez were used for official and literary purposes. In contrast, Sabaean and Greek were used in trade and diplomatic contexts.

The renowned kingdom, referred to as the land of punt and the land of the gods, holds a significant position as the lens through which the gods gaze upon the world. Located in this cool region are the sources of the Nile rivers, namely the Blue Nile and the life-giving rivers that flow into Kush and eventually reach Egypt. The strategic geography of the highlands of Africa revolves around these crucial points of control over water and the fertility of the land. Their importance cannot be underestimated, as the very existence of the dynasties in Khemite Egypt Mizraim depends on the kingdoms that control the Nile rivers.

Ethiopia Top/ Europe Bottom
South is Up

The Tabula Rogeriana, as it is called in English, was made by Arab geographer Muhammad al-Idrisi in 1154. The map was commissioned by Roger II of Sicily (r. 1130-1154) around 1138, and took nearly 15 years to complete. Eight copies of the original map survive. This 1929 facsimile by Konrad Miller includes transliterations of the original Arabic text.

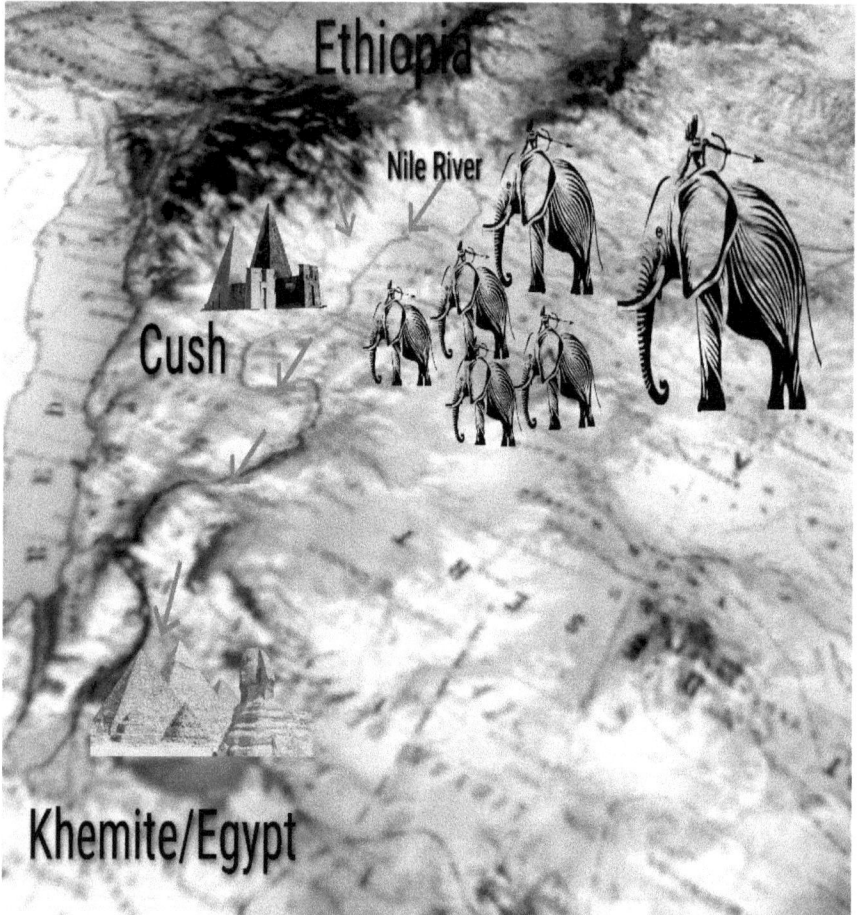

Topographical map of South up the Nile.
Egypt downstream/ elephants sub-Saharan abundance.

Egypt lies downstream, while Nubia Kush Ethiopia resides upstream. Ancient maps consistently place Kush and the headwaters of the Nile at the top, highlighting their significance. Moreover, this region is notable for being the home to the oldest known fossils of humanity, adding to its historical and archaeological significance. Occupied since prehistoric times, this area has maintained its presence to this day.

47

Francesco Solimena (1657-1747)
Allegoria dell'Africa
African woman/children/lion and Mounted African War Elephant African in the distance.

Diodorus Siculus,
The Library of History, Books II.35 – IV.58, Translated by C.H. Oldfather, Harvard University Press, 2000 On the Ethiopians who dwell beyond Libya and their antiquities (Book III, chaps. 1-7)

"Now the Ethiopians, as historians relate, were the first of all men, and the proofs of this statement, they say, are manifest. For that, they did not come into their land as immigrants from abroad but were natives of it and so justly bear the name of "autochthones" is, they maintain, conceded by practically all men; furthermore, that those who dwell beneath the noon-day sun were, in all likelihood, the first to be generated by the earth, is clear to all; since, since it was the warmth of the sun which, at the generation of the universe, dried up the earth when it was still wet and impregnated it with life, it is reasonable to suppose that the region which was nearest the sun was the first to bring forth living creatures. And they say that they were the first to be taught to honor.

the gods and to hold sacrifices and processions and festivals and the other rites by which men honor the deity; and that in consequence, their piety has been published abroad among all men, and it is generally held that the sacrifices practiced among the Ethiopians are those which are the most pleasing to heaven. As a witness, they call upon the poet, perhaps the oldest. Indeed, he was the most revered among the Greeks, for in the Iliad, he represents both Zeus and the rest of the gods with him as absent on a visit to Ethiopia to share in the sacrifices and the banquet which were given annually by the Ethiopians for all the gods together: For Zeus had yesterday to Ocean's bounds Set forth to feast with Ethiopia's faultless men, And he was followed there by all the gods. They state that, because of their piety towards the deity, they manifestly enjoy the favor of the gods since they have never experienced the rule of an invader from abroad, for from all time, they have enjoyed a state of freedom and peace one with another, and although many and powerful rulers have made war upon them, not one of these has succeeded in his undertaking. "

This one statement alone declares the impenetrable might of Ethiopia Kush as Kings and guardians of the South Land of God.

Francesco Solimena (1657-1747)
Allegoria dell'Africa

One cannot overlook the role of documentation in understanding the region. It is not merely about well-documented history but also about protecting and preserving this documentation. Multiple institutions worldwide safeguard valuable records, and at the center of this dynamic lies the Quran, a sacred scripture revered by many and regarded as the most feared and respected among the world's religions. Islam, in this context, is credited with safeguarding the documentation rather than the exports of the people of Ethiopia. The ethnicities and specific details of the region's inhabitants have been meticulously documented and continue to be preserved, leaving no room for misinterpretation or detachment from their historical context.

Even if some attempt to distort the general representation of pure African ancestries, particularly those of negroid origin, or undermine the importance of specific characters, these well-documented facts cannot be refuted or easily changed without significant conflict. It is within this historical and cultural context that a particular passage from the Quran, known as the Conductors of the Elephant, is recognized.

In the 105th chapter of the Koran, it reads: "Do you not know how God treated the conductors of the elephants? Did he not turn their own perfidy against them? He sent myriads of birds soaring over their heads Who threw stones graven upon them with celestial vengeance. The infidels were cut down like corn by the reapers."

Now, let me regale you with the saga of Abraha. In the year A.D. 569, Abraha, a mighty titan who ruled as Governor over Yemen and Ethiopia, unfurled the banner of war that stretched over a millennium, casting its imposing shadow across the ancient realms. During this epoch, a formidable dominion of distinct Hebrews held sway in Yemen, mercilessly persecuting the devoted Christians who dared to stand against them. The sovereign of those southern Hebrews, Dhu Nowas, brazenly orchestrated unspeakable horrors, including the conflagration of Christian sanctuaries, the desecration of the relics

of Saint Paul, and the fiery immolation of no fewer than 20,000 Christians. Such was the gruesome tableau painted by Dhu Nowas' reign.

Desperate and oppressed, the Christian faithful beseeched the great Roman Emperor Justinian, whose martial valor had been tried and found wanting in the Arabian furnace. Seeking counsel, Justinian turned to the venerable Patriarch of the Coptic Church in Alexandria, whose sagacious wisdom directed his gaze to none other than St. Elesbaan, the indomitable Emperor of Ethiopia.

In response, St. Elesbaan marshaled an indomitable legion of 70,000 fierce warriors, forging a bond of absolute trust with his unyielding general, Abraha, a man whose rise from the depths of servitude mirrored the phoenix's ascent from its ashes. The might of 150 naval behemoths carried Abraha's valiant legions across the formidable Red Sea, where the very coast of Yemen trembled beneath the weight of impending conflict. A clash of titans unfolded, a conflagration of battle that echoed the landing of Julius Caesar on the shores of Britain. The outcome was cast in the die of Abraha's favor, his forces trampling Dhu Nowas' dominion and tragically forever silencing the battle cries of 26,000 Hebrews of the Himyar Kingdom. Victorious, the Ethiopians' banner fluttered triumphantly over the captured bastion of Zhafar, wrestling even Dhu Nowas' cherished queen from his grasp. Despite the vanquished ruler's desperate attempts to rally, the fates remained resolute, driving him to meet his tragic end as he cast himself, defeated and broken, into the unforgiving abyss of the sea.

In the wake of victory, Abraha assumed the mantle of power over Yemen's dominion. The ministers of the fallen Jewish sovereign faced the unforgiving blade of his judgment, their ill-gotten wealth seized as a tribute to his irresistible prowess. A phoenix reborn, the church at Zhafar was resurrected from its ruins under Abraha's unwavering gaze. Yet, as history is wont to weave its enigmatic tapestry, the great St. Elesbaan, for reasons veiled in the shrouds of obscurity, found his satisfaction wane in the presence of Abraha's might. A Christian Arab,

Aryat by name, was anointed to supplant Abraha as governor, and a storm of indignation brewed in his heart.

An explosive clash ensued, where the clash of titans transformed into a personal vendetta. The arenas of combat played host to their singular strife, the climax reaching its zenith when Abraha's brow was etched with the scarlet brand of injury. Yet, his relentless spirit spurred him to persevere. Fate, a capricious mistress, intervened as Abraha's adversary, Aryat, met his doom at the hands of an obedient enslaved person, returning the scepter of power to Abraha's formidable grasp. "Scarface," they named him, an epithet that bore testament to his unassailable courage and the crimson badge of his resilience. Under his imperious reign, Yemen thrived as a realm basking in the aura of his supremacy.

Driven by a fervor to etch his mark upon the annals of time, Abraha embarked upon the monumental task of erecting a resplendent sanctuary in Sanaa, a beacon of splendor destined to draw pilgrims' eyes from distant lands. Marble, sourced from the vaults of the Roman Empire itself, became the very building blocks of his vision. And yet, his ambition knew no bounds; he endeavored to divert the tide of faithful pilgrims from the sanctified precincts of Mecca, an audacious venture that stirred the foundations of faith and trade among the Arabian denizens.

But the cauldron of discord brewed hotter with each passing day, the flames of resistance licking at the borders of Abraha's grand design. An Arabian soul, emboldened by fervent belief, confronted

Abraha's ambition with a visceral gesture of defiance. Upon the altar of Abraha's burgeoning edifice, this audacious soul deposited the refuse of his

body, a profound act of protest against Abraha's hegemony. The insult was profound, the response swift. Abraha, interpreting this as an unrelenting challenge, unleashed his fury, vowing to lay waste to the hallowed sanctuary of Mecca.

An expedition of grand proportions was marshaled, a fearsome tide of 40,000 warriors, cavalry, and behemoth elephants armored in golden armor and garments of silk and diverse African embroideries for the cataclysmic confrontation. The earth quaked beneath the advance of Abraha's juggernaut. destiny, that fickle mistress, cast her die. A tempest of swirling sand swallowed thousands of Abraha's stalwart soldiers, their valiance vanquished by the desert's merciless embrace. Pestilence, in the form of smallpox, ravaged the ranks of the faithful, a silent scourge that snuffed out life's spark in the blink of an eye.

And thus, Abraha stood upon the threshold of Mecca, a city poised to bow before his irresistible might. The crescendo of his conquest was nigh, a crescendo heralded by the majestic figure of "Mahmoud the Praiseworthy," a colossal white elephant adorned in the resplendence of silk and find colors of garments and gold stones and golden plated armor. Yet, destiny's script remained unwritten, for it halted as this living monument to Abraha's dominion passed beneath the arches of Mecca's gates. It stood its ground, immovable, unyielding. Some whispered of illness, of nerves trembling in the face of the unknown. Arab writers, bards of their fate, offered another account—that the elephant knelt, an act of defiance.

A chorus of jubilation erupted from the heart of the Arabian defenders, their hearts swelling with the conviction that a higher power had intervened, that their sacred city, their Mecca, was destined to stand untouched by the encroaching tide. At this moment, Abraha's power faltered, and the notoriety of his use, taming, and training of the African war elephant would never be forgotten.

But also a point to remember in this saga. It's evident to see the politics of the ancient world still to this day. And the play of religion and ancestry regarding

economics and geography. It would seem that a people with a focused place, an internationally recognized place of gathering to be honored and respected, and a place of storage of wealth and commerce for the prosperity of a people and their descendants, creates conflict. That place also becomes a target, as it is used to manipulate populations and transfer wealth to a centralized place for those in the surrounding regions to have first access. It would seem that every area of account or culture people should have a center place for themselves to be edified, restored, and celebrated, and thanks solely to their creator and thanks for their identities and ancestries on earth.

To this point of wealth and identity, the Axumite Empire is distinguished in history also in the garments of their warfare with warrior regalia as an exquisite ensemble that reflected the rich cultural heritage and martial prowess of the ancient Axumite Kingdom. The regalia consisted of various instruments and garments, each meticulously designed to inspire awe and intimidation on the battlefield. Here are detailed descriptions of some of the key components:

Pliny the Elder 79 AD
(The Book of natural History)
Book6: ch34

"So called from Azania, the adjoining coast of Africa, now known as that of Ajan. It was inhabited by a race of Æthiopians, who were engaged in catching and taming elephants, and supplying the markets of the Red Sea coast with hides and ivory."

"After King Kaleb defeated Fenhas (king of Yemen) he traveled back to Aksum, his capital being chariot."
The oxymite imperial Kaleb is transported on an Elephant-drawn chariot. There are some illustrations of chariots being pulled by four elephants and others by multiple elephants with royal canopy atop.

AFTER KING KALEB DEFEATED FINEHAS IS TRAVLI.1? HIS CAPITAL BEING CHARIOT.

Helmet (Nabele): The helmet worn by Axumite warriors was a magnificent piece crafted from intricately worked iron or bronze. It featured a high crest

adorned with feathers, symbolizing the warrior's rank and achievements. The helmet's faceplate often displayed intricate engravings depicting religious and mythological motifs.

Cuirass (Awraja): The cuirass was a breastplate made from overlapping iron or bronze scales. It covered the warrior's chest and upper abdomen, protecting them without compromising mobility. The scales were meticulously polished and sometimes decorated with ornate motifs, reflecting the warrior's status and affiliation.

Shield (Adis): The shield was a circular or oval-shaped wooden construction reinforced with leather or metal, intricately painted with vibrant colors and detailed patterns, often depicting mythical creatures or heroic scenes. The shield's central boss was adorned with polished metal studs, enhancing its defensive capabilities and aesthetic appeal.

Spear (Gerar): The spear was the primary weapon. It featured a long wooden shaft, typically made from durable acacia or ebony wood, affixed with a sharp, double-edged iron or bronze spearhead. The spearhead was intricately carved and decorated with engravings, symbols of power and protection.

Sword (Megaz): The Axumite sword symbolized honor and prestige. It had a straight, double-edged blade, usually measuring around 60 centimeters in length. The blade was forged from high-quality iron or steel, renowned for its strength and sharpness. The hilt was adorned with exquisite carvings and encrusted with gemstones or precious metals, indicating the warrior's social status.

Garments (Hamis): The garments Axumite warriors wore were practical and visually striking. They included a tunic-like shirt made from fine linen, often dyed in vibrant red, blue, or purple colors. The shirt featured intricate embroidery along the hem and collar, depicting traditional motifs and symbols. Over the shirt, warriors wore a sleeveless vest or jacket made from animal skins, such as leopard or lion, signifying their bravery and prowess.

Warriors adorned themselves with accessories like belts, arm bands, and anklets. These accessories were crafted from precious metals, such as gold or silver, and featured intricate patterns and gemstone embellishments. They also wore

feathered headdresses, symbolizing their connection with the divine and the spiritual realm.

LUCA GIORDANO (COPIAS) (NAPLES, ITALY, 1634- 1705)
Africa

Leopard skins and royal regalia played a significant role in the culture of the Axumite Empire. Leopard skins, in particular, held great symbolism and were associated with royalty and power. High-ranking individuals, including the king and nobility, often wore them as a symbol of their authority. With its distinctive pattern, the leopard skin conveyed a sense of prestige and awe.

In addition to leopard skins, the Axumite royalty adorned themselves with majestic royal regalia, including elaborate crowns and jewelry. These regal accessories were crafted with exquisite artistry, often incorporating precious metals, gemstones, and intricate designs. The regalia served as visual representations of the royal status and were worn on ceremonial occasions to emphasize the grandeur and majesty of the Axumite rulers.

Culturally, to this day, many of the East African cultures and ethnicities that existed during the time of Axum still practice traditional clothing and armor in specific ceremonies and historical celebrations. So much so that I cannot cover it in this first work; the second edition will distinctly address the greater issue of regalia...the missing regalia. Further in this book, we will consistently remind ourselves as readers and historians that the African war elephant regalia is missing. And it is not lost as well as it is no mistake. But these items are prized treasures among collectors and the families of kings. Many of these items mentioned in this book regarding the regalia of the African war elephant will never be seen by common eyes because the glory of ancient times was the glory of Africa and the power of the mounted prehistoric beasts of War.

Where are the relative elephant regalia pieces? The elephant tusk blades, the elephant headdressed, the elephant thrones, the elephant saddles, the elephant armors, the elephant towers, the elephant national fabrics of kush, of Khemite Egypt, of Mali, of Zulu, of Benin, of Zimbabwe, of Ethiopia., Where is the regalia? Who has it, and what museums are public or stored away deep in the halls of billionaire private museums, one of a kind with rare items never before photographed? Where are they?

Although we need to mention another historical figure of Ethiopia Axum named Bilad Al Habesha, We will do so in another segment regarding Mali. So, we will tell the final tale of Ethiopia from a Hebrew perspective by the story of Eldad Ha Dani. Because his narratives were born the tales of a mystical person named Prester John. Believed to be the great king of Ethiopia, to which the Europeans in the Middle ages desired to become an ally from the tales of the African King rappelling Muslim armies, my powers are unknown. Though now in history, it is believed that the entire narrative was framed and ordered to penetrate the South Realm. In the second edition of this book, we will highlight the Christian Hebrew kingdoms of Kush, The Kingdom of Makuria, The Kingdom of Alodia Kush and of the Islamic empires of Somalia the kingdom of Adal and the Kingdom of The Ajuran Sultanate ruling the horn of Africa.

"Eldad Ha Dani "
And
" The ancient Livite Jews in Ethiopia"

Eldad HaDani, known as the "Danite," is recorded to be recognized for belonging to the Tribe of Dan, one of The Hebrew people who became a kingdom after the fall of ancient Khemite—migrating to the east. Israel split into two kingdoms after King Solomon, Israel to the north and the Yahudi Kingdom in the South. The King Shalmaneser of Assyria invaded and besieged Samaria, leading to its fall three years later. The ten tribes believed to be exiled to Assyria seemingly vanished from history. However, according to Eldad, the Danite's account passed down through generations shows that the Ten Tribes did not vanish. Eldad conveyed that his tribe, the Danites, foresaw Assyria's growing might and their inevitable subjugation. Unwilling to fight brethren from Judah and foreseeing the Kingdom of the Ten Tribes' impending fall, the Danites opted to leave Israel. In 3191, during Ahaz's reign, they embarked on a journey to Kush/Ethiopia via Khemite/Egypt, establishing their kingdom in East Africa after overcoming native tribes. Later, the tribes of Naftali, Gad, and Asher joined the Danites.

Eldad revealed that these tribes communicated with the Sons of Moses across a river called Sambatyon, sending questions on parchment tied to pigeons. Eldad's lineage is traced back to Hushim, son of Dan, from whom all Danites descended. Notably, Samson hailed from their tribe. Their white banner bore the words "Hear O Israel," serving as a war cry.

Isolated from the larger Hebrew community, the four tribes remained unfamiliar with the eminent Jewish Sages, the Tannaim and Amoraim, who authored the Mishnah and the Gemara and lacked possession of the Talmud. Nevertheless, they steadfastly adhered to the Torah's laws and traditions. Their guidance came from their forebears and scholars who handed down teachings from one generation to another in an unbroken chain since Joshua and Moses.

Their elders ingrained it in them: "These are the words of Joshua, who received the Torah from Moses, who received the Torah from HaShem."

Eldad the Danite exclusively used Hebrew, asserting that his tribe and the other three spoke solely the Holy Tongue. Eldad recounted the tale of the Sons of Moses residing beyond the legendary River Sambation. His narrative unfolded as follows:

Following the destruction of the Beth-Hamikdosh and the Babylonian captivity of the Jews, the Chaldeans demanded that the Levite Sons of Moses, who were musicians in the temple, sing the songs of Zion. However, overcome with grief before HaShem, they lamented, "How can we sing HaShem's song on foreign soil?" As a solemn pledge, they wounded their fingers, vowing, "These fingers that once played flutes and harps within the temple shall not resound in impure lands."

Witnessing their anguish, Hashem dispatched a cloud to transport them, along with their families, possessions, sheep, and cattle, to Havilah, the fabled Land of Gold, under the cover of night. The noise of their arrival reverberated intensely through the night, reaching the ears of the Hebrews from the four tribes. Come dawn, they encountered their brethren, the Sons of Moses, who had recently landed nearby. Yet, a formidable river stood between them. The river's currents surged violently, propelling stones and spraying into the air with a thunderous clamor. This tumult persisted for a week, impeding all passage. With the arrival of Shabbat, the river was tranquilized, its waters assuming a serene repose. A dense cloud enveloped the water, barring access once again. This river was henceforth dubbed Sambatyon, signifying the "Shabbat River."

Eldad detailed his travels, including a shipwreck near cannibal-infested lands. He survived their captivity, subsequently being sold to a Jewish merchant in Yemen. Traveling through the Arabian Peninsula, he encountered various tribes, including Ephraim, Manasseh, Reuben, Issachar, Zebulun, and the city of Kairwan in North Africa. Upon his arrival in Kairwan, the Jewish community

questioned Eldad's credibility. They sought validation from Gaon Rabbi Zemach, head of a Babylonian Yeshiva, who confirmed much of Eldad's account, suggesting that his experiences had influenced his recollections. Eldad HaDani's captivating journey, as recounted in these records, brings to light the enduring tales of the Lost Tribes, their travels, and their role in preserving their legacy.

Ethiopians also used elephants to transport the massive stones to build the famous Obelisks of Aksum.

AAMSTERDAM,
Chez Wolfgang. Waesberge. Boom & van Someren, M.DC.LXXXVI.

John Ogiby

AFRICA: BEING AN ACCURATE DESCRIPTION OF THE REGIONS OF ÆGYPT, BARBARY, LYBIA, AND BILLEDULGERID, THE LAND OF NEGROES, GUINEE, ÆTHIOPIA, AND THE ABYSSINES, WITH ALL THE ADJACENT ISLANDS. COLLECTED AND TRANSLATED FROM MOST AUTHENTICK AUTHORS.
BY John Ogilvy 1670

This amazing artwork demonstrates quite a contrast between imagery and hidden history. We see Kushite African sitting at the seat of power, with a platformed throne and the cushite pyramids in the distance with the sun disk at the Pinnacle. We see all manner of beasts and types of people. We see the mounted war elephant, the right corner with the Warrior and spear, and two slaves in chains, which makes it look like you are being intimidated by a lion. As well as the ivory trade by the servant African next to the king illustrates an actual depiction and description of push as well as what is documented as the description above and an accurate depiction of Africa, Egypt library Libya, land of Negros Guinea, and Ethiopia.

Chapter 2
Kush

"Even if the elephant is thin, he is still the lord of the jungle."
~ African Proverb

Exert
-Evliya Çelebi Travels
"Evliya procession Up the Nile"

"Glory be to God, mountain and valley were filled with Bedouins. and numerous other people, marching wave on wave and regiment on regiment; thousands of elephants bearing guns and 300 mangonels, 6 Shahi bronze cannons and thousands of cannons made of elephant bones; myriads of camels bearing supplies; innumerable"

"**T**he world is upside down," I say again that the world is upside down. It is without question that Babylon is at the center of the ancient world and that the Semitic Afroasiatic histories of the world verifies that the first global king was The son of Kush. Anthropomorphically, allegorically, figuratively, or literally, Kush is synonymous with the

68

south, specifically the people spanning the African South, Arabian South, and Central and Southern Asia. As stated at the close of Chapter 1, the primary focus of this work is to highlight the interconnecting histories and linguistics of empires related to one another. My documentation and recognition. So what is here that the evidence of the use and timing of the Royal African Elephant are engraved in the hieroglyphics of the walls of Kush Nubia Meroe Kushite king riding an elephant (ca. 200 BCE-200 CE), Sudan. Source: E. A. Wallis Budge. The Egyptian Sudan: Its History and Monuments. Vol. 2

(London: K. Paul, Trench, Trübner, 1907), 150 fig. 6).
-Queen Amanirenas-

of Kush (Nubia): She led the Kushite resistance against Roman forces in the 1st century BCE and successfully defeated them in the (Meroetic Wars).

Queen Amanirenas of Kush (Nubia) is known for using war elephants during her resistance against Roman forces in the 1st century BCE. These war elephants have always been a crucial part of Kushitic Military Strategy. These African bush elephants and Desert Elephants are known for their size, strength, and ability to strike fear into the hearts of opponents. In fine Nubian Gold Armorer, intricately designed cloths and fabrics with towers made of wood and overlaid gold decorated with Nubian designs and craftsmanship and trained to carry archers or other soldiers into combat. War elephants were a common feature in ancient warfare, and their use by Queen Amanirenas irrefutably was a significant factor in her successful resistance against Roman incursions into Nubian territory. During Queen Amanirenas's resistance against Roman forces, the Roman general leading the campaign in Egypt was most likely Gaius Petronius. He was the Roman prefect of Egypt during the reign of Emperor Augustus (Octavian), the Roman Emperor at the time.

Gaius Petronius was responsible for the Roman campaigns in Egypt, including the conflict with Queen Amanirenas and the Kingdom of Kush during the Meroitic War in the 1st century BCE. Emperor Augustus, also known as Octavian, was the Roman Emperor from 27 BCE to 14 CE and played a key role in the management of the Roman Empire during this period. Queen Amanirenas of Kush (Nubia) is known for her clever arrangement of war elephants on the battlefield during the Meroitic War against Roman forces. Her strategic use of these elephants and the formation she employed were designed to strike fear into the Romans and create an impenetrable front to the point of her formation arrangement being an impenetrable formation to end fear rather than even attempt

after all the miles traveled through the desert. What shall we say then to this point? Obviously, this tactic would go down in history, and her formation of war elephants, military acumen, and fierce warriors played a significant role in her successful resistance against the Romans during this conflict.

Animals and Nubians at the Alexandra Palace

The image of Nubian warriors adorned in golden armor, wielding golden spears and shields while commanding mighty war elephants in a strategically impeccable formation, is most certainly powerful and captivating. Such a spectacle on the battlefield was awe-inspiring and undoubtedly struck fear into the hearts of the Romans. The combination of military might, skilled tactics and the dazzling display of wealth and power would have made Queen Amanirenas's forces a formidable and

formidable adversary. Stories of kings and warriors using reflective shields or armor on the battlefield to manipulate sunlight as a tactical advantage are not uncommon in various cultures and historical accounts. Such stories often blend elements of strategy, psychology, and folklore. Here's a general outline of what these stories typically entail:

The Use of Reflective Shields or Armor: A king or warrior is equipped with specially designed shields or armor in these stories. These shields or armor are often polished or made from materials with a reflective surface.

Sunlight as a Weapon: During a battle, the warrior or king positions themselves strategically so that the reflective surfaces of their shields or armor catch and focus sunlight

Blinding the Enemy: By angling the reflective surface towards the enemy, they direct the intense beams of sunlight into the eyes of their opponents.

Psychological Impact: The blinding effect of the reflected sunlight disorients and blinds the enemy soldiers, causing confusion and panic among their ranks.

Advantageous Positioning: The king or warrior, taking advantage of the chaos, may launch an attack, advance their position, or achieve a tactical advantage while the enemy is temporarily blinded and unable to defend effectively.

The stories are often passed down as legends or folklore, making it challenging to determine whether they were used as actual military tactics or symbolic narratives meant to highlight the brilliance of African Warrior Kings and Queens. These stories add a captivating dimension to the history of warfare and strategy.

'1880 exotic animals brought back to African market"

Piankhy (Piye):

- Reign: Around 747–716 BCE
- Piankhy's legacy is etched with the hallmark of Nubia's regal tradition. Mounted on war elephants adorned with vibrant colors that resonated with the linens of Nubia, his campaigns, including the pivotal Battle of Eltekeh in 721 BCE, embodied the grandeur of a civilization that wielded both martial prowess and artistic sophistication.

2. Shabaka
- Reign: Around 721–707 BCE
- Shabaka's era resonates with the undeniable fact that Nubians adorned themselves in gold armor. Their regalia, akin to the richly hued fabrics that graced their homeland, converged with the ornate trappings of war elephants, creating a visual spectacle that stood as a testament to Nubia's unwavering cultural identity.

Taharqa
- Reign: Around 690–664 BCE
- Taharqa, a luminary of Nubian heritage, donned the distinctive gold armor synonymous with his people. As his war elephants traversed the battleground, their elaborate colors not only echoed the linens of Nubia but also encapsulated the essence of a civilization that fused military might with artistic finesse.

Tanutamun
- Reign: Around 664–656 BCE
- Tanutamun, like his predecessors, donned the revered gold armor, embodying Nubia's resplendent tradition. The vibrant colors adorning his war elephants echoed the palette of Nubian linens of cultural identity onto the canvas of the battlefield.

Taharqa, a significant Nubian pharaoh reigning around 690 to 664 BCE, is notable for deploying war elephants during military campaigns. Historical records affirm their involvement in battles, particularly against the Assyrian Empire. Accompanied by skilled warriors, these elephants bolstered Taharqa's military strategies, with their symbolic role in representing strength remaining evident and intertwined with Nubia's cultural identity.

Taharqa's military engagements with the Assyrians are well-documented, showcasing his efforts to defend Egypt and his native Nubia. These confrontations are integral to his historical narrative, illuminating his stance against powerful adversaries. Further emphasizing his significance, Taharqa is also mentioned in the Bible's book of 2 Kings 19:9, referred to as "Tirhakah, king of Cush." This reference highlights his involvement in the complex regional dynamics of his time, notably in the conflict between the Assyrian king Sennacherib and King Hezekiah of Judah. Throughout these reigns, the Nubian pharaohs wielded the legacy of their gold armor and elaborate colors with unwavering pride. Their war elephants, bedecked in resplendent hues reminiscent of Nubia's textile artistry, carried them into the annals of history as exemplars of a civilization that celebrated martial strength and aesthetic opulence.

The Meroitic script was used in inscriptions and texts in the Kingdom of Kush, particularly in Meroe, a prominent center of culture and administration. The script is characterized by its unique symbols and structure. Notably, the Meroitic language and script are distinctly African. In terms of related languages, the Nubian languages, part of the Nilo-Saharan language family, are often associated with the region's broader linguistic context. These languages, including Old Nubian and modern Nubian dialects, have been spoken in the

Nile Valley region, including parts of modern Sudan and Egypt. The Meroitic script makes it challenging to establish direct links. The Kushites used the Meroitic script to write the Meroitic language, and this distinctly African script and language showcase the cultural and linguistic diversity of the African continent. Within the second edition of this book, we will address the migrations of the Kushite ancestries into the Arabian peninsula and identify them as they are still present in DNA. It also addresses Nubia Kush's linguistics, the relationship between Kush and Khemitic, and the expansion to Western Africa in multitudes of migrations spanning millennia to the north, southeast, and west.

Additionally, the semantic literature identifies Kush as the ancestor of Nimrod in the Hebrew Bible. It is recognized as the first King to which all traditions of regalia of war, garments, quit proceedings, ceremony processions, formations, and the dispersion of people worldwide after once being unified under Kushite rulership of the World. In the Hebrew scriptures, the details are not related, but they are insinuated. The other Semitic kinds of literature are the details in the books of Jasher, which the book of Jasher is mentioned in the Hebrew Bible, giving it validity. The Book of Jasher is mentioned in Joshua 10:12-13 when the Lord stopped the sun in the middle of the day during the battle of Beth Horon. It is also mentioned in 2 Samuel 1:18-27 as containing the Song or Lament of the Bow, that mournful funeral song David composed at the time of the death of Saul and Jonathan. Henceforth, we can conclude that the book of Jasher is relevant and valuable in the historical context of regional, tribal, traditional, folklore, legend, and symbolic history.

The book of Jasher is of great significance because it details the city of Babylon and the kingdom of Iraq under the rulership of Kushites, to which Abraham's family was of the royal court. Abraham is not a direct Cushite but a relative (a cousin) to the Cushite family tree of all humanity

relative to the three main descendants after the global calamity of the flood. This will be addressed in the next chapter relative to the national lineages and branches of the African kingdoms of Kush.

Al-Hasan Ibn Muhammad Ibn Ahmad al-Wazzan Book III cht27

(From Book VII of A Geographical Historie of Africa, Written in Arabicke and Italian by Iohn Leo a More, born in Granada and brought up in Barbarie. Translated and collected by Iohn Pory (London:1600), pp. 295-296:)

"NUBIA bordering westward upon the kingdom last described [Gaoga], and stretching from thence unto Nilus, is enclosed on the south side with the desert of Goran, and on the north side with the confines of Egyp, howbeit they cannot pass by water from this kingdom into Egypt: for the river of Nilus is in some places no deeper then a man may wade over on foot. The principal town of this kingdom, called Dangala, is exceedingly populous and contains ten thousand families. The walls of their houses consist of a kind of chalke, and the roofs are covered with straw. The townspeople are exceedingly wealthy and civil and have significant traffic with the merchants of Cairo & Egypt. In other parts of this kingdom, you shall find none but villages and hamlets situated upon the river of Nilus, all the inhabitants of whom are husbandmen. The kingdom of Nubia is rich in corn and sugar, which they do not know how to use. Also, in the city of Dangala, there are plenty of civets and sandall wood. This region abounds with ivory likewise because there are so many elephants taken. Here is also the strongest and deadly poison, one grain of which, divided amongst ten persons, will kill them all within less than a quarter of an hour: but if one man taketh a grain, he dieth thereof out of hand. An ounce of this poison is sold for a hundred ducates;

neither may it be sold to any but to foreign merchants, & whosoever buyeth it is bound by oath not to use it in the kingdom of Nubia. All such as buy of this poison are constrained to pay as much unto the king as the merchant: but if any man selleth poison without the prince's knowledge, he is presently put to death.

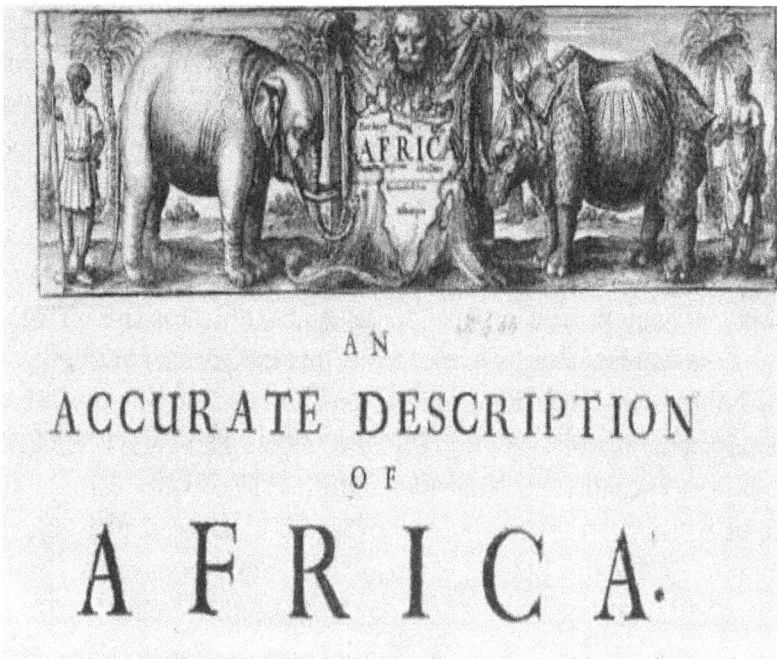

John Ogilby (1600-1676) published books with illustrations by Wenceslaus Hollar

The king of Nubia maintaineth continual warre, partly against the people of Goran (who being descended of the people called Zingani, inhabit the deserts, and speak a kind of language that no other nation understandeth) and partly against certain other people also dwelling upon the desert which lieth eastward of Nilus, and stretcheth towards the red sea, being

not far from the borders of Suachen. Their language (as I take it) is mixt, for it hath great affinity with the Chaldeann toong, with the language of Suachen, and with the language of Ethiopia the higher, where Prete Gianni is said to beare rule: the people themselves are called Bugiha and are most base and miserable, and live only upon milk, camels-flesh, and the flesh of such beasts as are taken in those deserts.

Sometimes, they receive the tribute of the governor of Suachen and sometimes of the governors of Dangala. They once had a rich town situate upon the red sea called Zibid, whereunto belonged to a commodious haven opposite the haven of Zidem, forty miles distant from Mecca. But a hundred years since the Soldan destroyed it, because the inhabitants received specific wares which should have been carried to Mecca, and at the same time, the famous port of Zibbid was destroyed, from whence notwithstanding was gathered a tremendous yearly tribute.

The inhabitants being chased from thence fled unto Dangala and Suachin, and at length being overcome in battle by the governor of Suachin, there were in one-day slaine of them above fower thousand, and a thousand were carried captive unto Suachin, who the women and children of the city massacred. And thus much (friendly reader) as concerning the land of Negros: the fifteen kingdoms of which agreeing much in rites and customs, are subject unto fower princes only. Let us now proceed to the description of Egypt.

Before we read any further into the names of tribes and people's and kingdoms and families, in no way are the references cited to insinuate any superiority or inferiority of one belief or culture against another. Seeing that it is the story of humanity relative to us ourselves that tells us we are one family of many branches, disciplines, and respects. This

disclaimer is necessary; although it was not stated in the introduction, it is appropriate to emphasize this information point. Furthermore, it is important to indicate a separation of appreciation of historically documented evidence separate from cultural-based influenced bias in this field of study and literature.

The first dynasty of Kushite ancestry among scholars is up for debate. It was seen mainly because the stories of origin vary from culture to culture, which amazingly ties into the allegory of the mixing of language related to Babylon. Although there are key fundamental aspects to the Cushite origins of civilization, we will only touch on a few as we progress. Further deepening the knowledge of the globalization of Kush civilizations, the monumental Hebrew Bible verse related to Kush is that his name was globally renownedn and a statement on the earth.

In the previous chapter and introduction, we emphasized that allegory, narrative, and the implication of control within a cultural the societal group occurs to generate a unifying national perspective that creates an agreed-upon valued lesson that implies good and evil, right and wrong, winning and losing, life and death. It is apparent that from the earliest civilizations, there has been an instinct to project a provisional perspective related to the individual's or the group's survival and identity.

Defining the story and the parameters of the values are indicated in the national stories and perspectives of a people to which they pass the lessons learned and battles fought. Please take a moment to digest what we have just established. Understanding the key interpretations of ancestral stories and folklore of names, places, and people to be taught and in a specific manner to be easily remembered and retained was how

the ancients passed down information because most civilizations were not literary-based.

Critical information was translated into poetic stories that contained the values. But we will touch on this further in discussion. Concerning the name of Kush, we see this in the similarities of the name in the sound and spelling of Kush and even What is accepted to be the first ruling king, Nimrod, and Namer Menas. And should not be considered just a coincidence.

Although it can become more confusing in people redefining themselves, in the changing of a name, or The naming of events given to children. As it often occurs within the premise of battles, it is the renaming and claiming of territories and families after defeat in conflict. We'll also address this further in the next segment.

An elephant and war captives form a temple frieze near Meröe, first century AD. Elephants were used for military and ceremonial purposes at Kush/Meröe.

"Looking closely at the details you can see the intricate designs of the linens and cushidic armorings and designs along the sides of the rear to the elephant and prisoners walking in front of the elephant procession, originally there are a multitude and line of elephants in a procession, but the others are indistinguishable but present" Ancient Nubian Tribes of Kush: Kerma, The Kerma people were prominent within the heartland of Kush, known for their significant cultural and architectural contributions. Nobatae, The Nobatae inhabited northern Nubia, near Egypt, and played a role in the interactions between Nubia and its neighboring regions.

"1880 exotic animal trade Nubian market"

Blemmyes: The Blemmyes were situated within the heart of Nubia and contributed to the region's diverse cultural landscape.

Medjay: The Medjay were a Nubian tribe known for their role as skilled archers and warriors in ancient Egypt, often serving as elite forces.

Makurians: The Makurians resided in the Kingdom of Makuria, an important Nubian kingdom in the region.

Ballana, The Ballana people inhabited areas along the Nile in what is now Sudan and were part of the ancient Nubian milieu.

Argo: The Argo tribe was part of the broader cultural fabric of Nubia, contributing to the region's rich heritage.

Irtjet: The Irtjet people were integral to the societal dynamics of ancient Nubia, shaping its historical narrative.

Karmah: The Karmah tribe's presence added to the cultural mosaic that defined the ancient Nubian civilization.

Panhesy: The Panhesy tribe was a significant part of the Nubian identity of the region.

Tribes Expanding into Arabia and Ethiopia
The Hadhramaut Tribe Originating from Kus: The Hadhramaut tribe migrated to the Arabian Peninsula, particularly the Hadhramaut region in

present-day Yemen. Their migration enriched the Arabian Peninsula with Nubian heritage, adding a layer of cultural diversity to the region.

The Nobatae As mentioned earlier, the Nobatae tribe had a presence in northern Nubia. Elements of the Nobatae people migrated into the Ethiopian landscape, contributing to the interwoven cultural connections between Nubia and Ethiopia.

R1*

According to a study by Clyde Ahmed Winters with Research Gate on the High Blood Group DNA of r1 as a Founding Kushite Ancestry, the history of the ancient Kushite civilization reveals a remarkable tale of expansion, cultural influence, and connections across vast distances. The legacy of the Kushites, also known as Ethiopians, is interwoven with their migration from Africa to Asia, leaving an indelible mark on history. Through evidence gleaned from historical texts, archaeological discoveries, and linguistic analysis, the story of the Kushite expansion emerges as a testament to their enduring impact.

Herodotus, an ancient Greek historian, provides a crucial link to this tale, claiming to have derived information from the Egyptians about the Kushites. Known also as Ethiopians, the term "Ethiopian" itself bears a unique meaning, arising from the Greek words "Ethios" and "ops," which combine to signify "burnt faces." This serves as a cultural marker, reflecting the dark-skinned individuals of this civilization. Classical literature further solidifies this connection by referring to the vast region stretching from Egypt to India as "Ethiopia," underscoring the scope of their influence.

These are segments of a chapter-by-chapter summary, with occasional notes of the Histories of Herodotus, based mainly on the translation by Peter Greene (1987), with occasional reference to translations by A.D. Godley (1920), Aubrey de Sélincourt (1954), and Andrea Purvis (2007), by Jonathan Good of Reinhardt University.

2:43

"Heracles is one of the twelve Gods in Egypt. The Greeks learned of Heracles from the Egyptians. H. has many proofs of this."

2:44

"H. sailed to Tyre in Phoenicia and Thasos, a Tyrian colony. Each place has shrines to Heracles, both older than the Greek Heracles. Thus, there are two Heracles: the ancient god and the hero. Those who have established separate cults to these two figures are correct to do so."

2:45

"One Greek story of Heracles is false, that he came to Egypt and they wanted to sacrifice him, so he slaughtered them all. But the Egyptians only sacrifice certain animals. How would they sacrifice humans? And how could a human kill so many people single-handedly?"

2:50

"The "names" (i.e., personalities) of nearly all the Greek gods derive from Egypt."

3:21

'The king of the Ethiopians saw through their ostensible gifts. He gave them a bow and said that they can remain in their land until the Persians can draw it."

3:23

"The Ethiopians live to 120 on average. They eat boiled meat and drink milk. Their great age derives from a fountain. The water is light (nothing floats in it) and sweet smelling; if you wash it, your skin is smoothed. The king showed them his dungeon of prisoners bound in gold chains (bronze is their most valuable metal). He also showed them the Table of the Sun."

Title cartouche of the map of Africa by C. A'llard, c. 1696

This illustration and depiction on this map is undoubtedly one of the most profound descriptions of cushite military culture and advanced Warfare. Depiction of a beautiful African princess of noble lineage and the pyramids of Kush In the background with three mounted War elephants with driver and archers. Kush being renowned as "Ta Seti" Land of the Bow!

Historical records unveil a tapestry of interactions between the Kushites, Africa, and Asia. Dr. Hansberry's research highlights the compelling evidence of African Kushites ruling across these continents. This dominion resonates in ancient scholars' accounts of

the first rulers of Elam, with Strabo, an ancient geographer, asserting that the founder of the first Elamite colony at Susa was Tithonus, a King of Kush. The very citadel bore the name "Memnonium," a testament to this Kushite legacy.

The intricate connections between language and culture are laid bare as the Elamite language is shown to be closely related to Dravidian and Niger-Congo languages. These linguistic ties reveal the intricate threads that link Africa, Arabia, and India. Genetic studies and linguistic analyses further bolster this notion, suggesting an African origin for Dravidian speakers in India. The movement of people becomes evident in the presence of shared cultural traits, symbolized by the presence of Black-and-Red Ware (BRW) that spread across Nubia, Arabia, Iran, and India. This pottery becomes a tangible artifact of their migratory journey.

The Kushite expansion echoes the radiating waves of culture and influence. The BRW, a hallmark of their civilization, serves as a silent ambassador across these lands. From its origins in Nubia, it traverses Mesopotamia and Iran, leaving its mark in South India. Such artifacts paint a vivid picture of a people on the move, carrying their culture and identity across regions.

This expansion isn't confined to the realms of archaeology alone; it's etched in place names and gods' appellations. The Kassites of Iran are a striking example, with their god "Kashshu" mirroring their name. Even India bears the imprint of this journey, with "Kishkinthai" harking back to an ancient Dravidian kingdom. Such instances of cultural transference across vast expanses underscore the profound impact of the Kushites.

The narrative broadens as we venture into the heart of Asia. The Armenians provided a bridge between Kush and the Parthians, referred to as "Kushans." Homer, Herodotus, and Strabo, eminent figures of antiquity, lend their voices to the chorus, terming southern Persia as "AETHIOPIA." The region east of Kerma resonates with the name "Kusan" in Greek and Roman writings, leaving no doubt of Kushite influence. The story of the Kushite expansion becomes truly fascinating as it unfolds across the diverse landscapes of culture and geography. The Kushites retained their identity as they journeyed from Middle Africa to Asia. This legacy extends beyond the physical realm, manifesting in gods, kings, and languages.

Even the Kings of Sumer, a civilization of great antiquity, were often referred to as the "Kings of Kush," underscoring the far-reaching influence of this remarkable civilization. Central Asia bears witness to a significant Kushite tribe known as Kushana, while the Kushans of China adopt the moniker "Ta Yueh-ti" or "the Great Lunar Race."

While the Kushite expansion may have occurred in a time obscured by the sands of history, its echoes resound across the ages. Through the lens of historical texts, archaeological treasures, and linguistic connections, we catch glimpses of a journey that transcends borders, cultures, and time. The war elephants they employed, symbols of power and conquest, become the living embodiment of their migrational era. In these 29 interwoven quotes, we find the threads of an epic tale—the Kushite expansion from Africa to Asia. From Herodotus' accounts to the etymology of "Ethiopian," from the movements of ancient rulers to the spread of BRW, the story becomes clear: a migration that shaped the course of history. The enduring legacy of the Kushites reminds us of the intricate web that connects our world, bridging continents, cultures, and civilizations.

AFRICA 1710 N. VISSCHER II & P. SCHENK LARGE ANTIQUE
ENGRAVED MAP 18TH CENTURY

An African woman depicted riding on an African elephant and two
warriors in the distance. Pyramids of Kush depicted giving notation to the
region of Kush.

The modern Nubian tribes in Sudan, along with the Beja people:

Dongola: The Dongola tribe resides in northern Sudan, along the Nile. They are known for their cultural heritage and historical significance.

Halfaweyen: This tribe is found in the northern regions of Sudan, close to the Egyptian border. They have a rich cultural heritage that reflects the Nubian traditions.

Mahas: The Maha's tribe is centered around Wadi Halfa in northern Sudan. They have maintained their distinct cultural practices and are part of the broader Nubian community.

Kenzi: The Kenzi tribe is prominent around Aswan in Egypt and northern Sudan. They share cultural ties with other Nubian tribes in the region.

Sukkot: The Sukkot tribe resides in the northern regions of Sudan, near the border with Egypt. They are known for their contributions to Nubian culture and heritage.

Ababda: Although primarily found in Egypt, the Ababda tribe extends into northern Sudan. They have a nomadic lifestyle and are traditionally known for their trade and transportation skills.

Batta: The Batta tribe is located in northern Sudan and has a rich history intertwined with the Nile River and its surrounding areas.

Saraqna: The Saraqna tribe resides in the northern regions of Sudan and has contributed to Nubia's cultural tapestry.

Sikoot: The Sikoot tribe is known for its presence in northern Sudan, near the border with Egypt. They are part of the wider Nubian community.

Abu Hamad: The Abu Hamad tribe is situated along the Nile River and is known for its river connections and resources.

Shellal: The Shellal tribe is located in the northern regions of Sudan, contributing to the cultural mosaic of Nubia.

Ibrahimiya: The Ibrahimiya tribe is part of the Nubian communities in Sudan, preserving their cultural heritage.
Beja: The Beja people are a prominent ethnic group in the northeastern regions of Sudan, Egypt, and Eritrea. Known for their unique language and nomadic lifestyle, they contribute to the cultural

diversity of the region. These are about a few of the people of Sudan today of the most notable of history.

Exert Al Bakri
(1028-1094 A.D.) 1067 A.D.
(Description of the Qos-'Aydhāb Route)

"From this Oasis (al-Wāḥ) to the other two outer Oases (al-wahāyn al-khārijayn), there are three stopping places. There, the country of Islam ends. There are six stopping-places across the desert between six stopping-places across t. (Ar.Ist. I, II, p. 149).

The regions (kuwar) of Miṣr, Nūba, Dunqula (MC 7 30 r)

The town of Qos is situated on the bank of the Nile between Aswān and Akhmim. The distance between it [Qos] and Aswān is a three-day journey. It is a big town with extensive ancient ruins (āthār). Between Qos and Aswān, there are caverns excavated in the mountains, where there are tombs of dead from which [piss] asphalt (al-mūmyā) of good quality is extracted. They find this in the decayed bones (rimam) and between the shrouds of the dead [p. 243]. It is said that in the desert, which stretches from Qos to Aswān, there is a mountain with a mine of green emeralds (az-zumurrud al-akḥdar). But the danger arising from the fear of the Bujāh, the Nūba, and other tribes of Nuba and Arabs who dwell in those plains prevents [travelers] from visiting the mine, besides the fact that the caverns of that desert are distant and sanded up, and have been abandoned because of their remoteness from any inhabited country. (MC 730 v).

Aswān is the last town of Islam and a defense post for the [other] cities of Egypt. It has connections with Nubia. (MC 730 v).

Between Aswān and the town of Sūrī (? or Surā? Sawrā)<ref>All the Arab writers mention "al-Qaṣr" as the first Nubian locality. Probably "Sūrī" is a misreading for "al-Qasr." </ref>, where the territory of Nubia begins, there is a desert inhabited by nomads (a'rāb) called Banī Jamāl, Banī Hilāl, Banī Kināna, and Banī Juhaina: they pay tithes to the Lord (sahīb) of Egypt.

At Aswān begins the desert, which extends as far as the coast of the Red Sea (bahr an-Na'm, or b. an-nu'm) to a town on the Red Sea called ʿAdhdhāb.<ref>"Adhdhāb" is consistently found in the printed editions of Al-Bakri instead of ʿAydhāb.</ref> It is a desert in which various

tribes of the Sūdān, such as the Beja, roam. The mosque of an-nardīnī (ar-rudaynī)<ref>A misreading of the Arabic script of ar-rudaynī." </ref> is the last post dependent on Aswan and a station for Aswan's horses (ribāt). (MC 730 v).

[The route from Aswan to 'Adhdhāb]

'Adhdhāb is a town lying on the western coast of the sea. It is an embarkation port for 'the pilgrims, for [p. 244] those who go to Yemen and in other directions. It is inhabited by a tribe called Banī Būlos: it is said that these belong to the Bujāh, but others claim that they are related to the Arabs and that they are the Marāzīyyah, a section which Abū Bakr as-Siddīq expelled.

From 'Adhdhāb to Aswān, there are two routes: one is called Al-Waḍaḥ and is an 18-day journey across deserts and barren sands. These sands contain a little water; they are loose sands, blown by the winds so that the tracks are quickly effaced, and nobody can take the correct direction on a footpath or a track; camelmen themselves travel on this desert trusting their she-camels which feel the route, and allow themselves to be guided by them. The other route is called after al-'Allāqī, which is also 18 stations and completely isolated. It is named after a river bed (nahr) called 'Allāqī. This town is rich with pomegranates and produces them in abundance: it also has many inhabitants who claim descent from the Arab tribe of Kalb ibn Wabrah. They behave properly with travelers and protect them.

Most of the mountains along this road contain gold and silver mines. The mountains that are of difficult access are inhabited by the Bujāh, some of whom are Muslims, and trade with those who happen to pass through that region.

Fromhāb and Ra's al-Maldam, elephants and gi, in this plain To the west of Aswān, lies the island of Bilāq, surrounded by the Nile; on it, there is a town with a mosque and Muslim townspeople from the country of Miṣr and Aswān. This island is situated in a place called the Cataracts (al-Janādil). (Ar.Ist. II, pp. 167 - 168; MC fol. 730 v.)."

As stated before, the world is upside down, and to understand this better is to understand the ancient world. The earliest mapping and cartography is seen with the south as the top because animal migration to warm climates is the direction of hunting and vegetation. And the Hebrew scriptures declared Nimrod, the son of Kush, to be a mighty hunter. Here is the relationship of Kush to Nimrod and Kush Nubia / Meroetic Kings and the semitic connections of the Axumite empire.

Axum defeated Kush and destroyed the city of Meroe from the direction of the south. The origin story related to the kingdom of Kush, according to scholarship, is unrelated to Egypt and distinct, but the origin story of the Egyptians is that they originated from the south, clearly saying that Egypt and Kush are relative people, according to Egyptian history. Still, the information on Kush itself is in pieces. However, the semitic Hebrew literatures state that they are the same ancestral family. So, understanding the origin of Egypt is to understand the origin of Kush and the dominant geography of the land, which puts the southern territory of the Highlands in the militarily dominant position. Kush Ethiopia is the higher ground with the access guarding the south and the life-giving waters of the Nile pouring down from the south of Kush into Egypt, however, according to modern egyptology scholarship. The first Kushite king chosen to recognize is King Alara, a King of Kush who is the first recorded prince of Nubia, founded the Napatan, or Twenty-fifth, Kushite dynasty at Napata in Nubia, now Sudan. Alara's successor, Kashta, extended Kushite control north to Elephantine and Thebes in Upper Egypt.

Kashta's successor, Piye, seized control of Lower Egypt around 727 BCE, creating the Twenty-fifth Dynasty of Egypt.

When looking at a map and understanding ancient world geography, you will see why upper Egypt, according to today's maps, is at the bottom, and lower Egypt is toward the Mediterranean, and it's understood why the ancient maps place the south as the top, because to go to Egypt, from the Mediterranean, is to go up, and to go from Egypt to Kush, is to go up higher.

Events become lessons learned that represent principles of value, that become names with specific meanings of events, or values that become lessons learned, and pass down as myths, that embody principles that become names, and these names are given to children, within a culture these names, represent values. Which oftentimes as we have seen within cultures. Leaders and kings often rename themselves or choose names that carry specific meanings, which is why people oftentimes in history have multiple names associated with specific events or principles within the culture. As in the name Nimrod, his name became renowned in the world before the language became multiple languages in the Hebrew culture. His name came to mean "we rebel" which we will touch on in the next chapter cultures rename and change the values of other opposing cultures, and even within a culture changes, of dialect, principles mutate, and transform into different sounds as well as different meanings.

Search
Musawwarat es-Sufa, Temple of Apedemak, Relief of an elephant and P.O.W.s

Regardless of any cultural background, bias to the validity of scripture or the names or to the realities of people as literal people or as mythological

allegories created to be lessons taught and told. Kush as we know it, according to world history was a true group of people. Regardless, it was an individual singular living breathing person. The reality is that a group of human ancestry called themselves kushites and have been known to be kushites and dominate the southern hemisphere of the world.

The Hebrew literature of the book of Jasha in collaboration with the Hebrew Bible does state that Nimrod was the son of Kush and the kingdom began in Iraq and the building of a city called Shinar which today are real literal places and is accepted through history. And the book of Jasha relates that Nimrod the son of Kush was its king and extended family members to whom early man was closely related. Just as in today's villages and tribes of older cultures, people are closely related and some villages completely are all relatives. But in the court of Nimrod was Abraham's father and his family which is a mirror type of the same story of the birth of Christ being born with a prophecy and a star marking the birth of Abraham, we will address the similarities of events, signifying births and new ages further in discussion. Interestingly, in the book of Jasha, Abraham's father, Tara had 12 sons and one named after each month of the zodiac.

The pivotal point of the story that is shared in the book of Jasher that is not mentioned in the other scriptures is that Nimrod had been given the clothing of Adam, who was the direct son of God for whom God made clothing and covered him with animal skins. And the story goes on to state that Khem, the third son of Noah, had stolen the clothing from Noah and given it to his son, Kush, and Kush had given it to Nimrod and these garments of skins gave Nimrod power beyond the natural world and within the natural world and great renown in the earth and no one could defeat him. Thus, he dominated the entire known world at the time and

became the world's first king, and in his courts were his relatives and descendants of Shem, and descendants of Khem and Yapeth. All was subject to him.

Nimrod's subjugation of the world took a term for the worse in a rebellion of his leadership that God saw fit to dismantle by the confusion of communication of all the people's unity in the separations of languages throughout the world and from there the empire of Kush and mankind dispersed and disconnect but some stayed to which Abraham's family remained loyal to Nimrod, the son of Kush. But the story of Abraham took several specific turns, causing him to have a revelation and hide away from his life for his protection as Nimrod, having heard of his birth sought out to kill him, but his father Tara lied to Nimrod and presented to him a child of a slave that Nimrod believed was Abraham. After the revelation of many years, Abraham made himself known to Nimrod and after several miracles of divine intervention, Abraham left the house of his father for the land of Canaan to which the story of Abraham and the Hebrew scriptures begins to unfold.

Kush, Cush, Kushi, Cushim, Cushite, Kusheti, Chalde Chaldean, Chaldeas, Keith Kusumita, Kushala, Kush, Kusuma, Kushali, Kusuo, Kusagra, Kusner, Kusum are all different forms of the name stretching from Ethiopia and also remembering the Ethiopian traditions that Kush had a son named Ethiopia to which, according to some traditions these are the origins of the son named Axum. But these different forms of the word Kush without a doubt, indicate the ancestral dispersion to the ends of Asia. The connection between the garments mentioned in the book of Jasha Adam being given to Kush, and being given to Nimrod is that they are the coats of animal skins for which Kush is most notable on the hieroglyphic walls of Kush and Kemite in the wearing of animal skins of

leopard hide as the signature garment of Kush and to know these realities or profound and that the entire system of royal ceremonies and processions were set in order by Nimrod according to the literature. And it is the scattering of the nations and the stretching across to Ethiopia/ the Ethiopia of modern-day Africa, Highlands and Nubia that are relative to known ancestries and the customs closest related and the leading Kushite families from ancient times up until the fall of Kush at the hands of Axum.

And to follow the historical narrative given in the Bible in the book of Genesis chapter 10 giving the table of nations as one of the most important scriptures in the Bible that give a real reference to active empires of the days of old in the region. The Hittites and Kushites, Khemites, Canaanites all African cultures and bloodlines families of Khem. According to biblical accounts, Nimrod is described as the son of Cush. This places Nimrod and, by extension, the association with the Kingdom of Kush in a timeframe that predates the classical period of Ancient Greece. The biblical narrative suggests an early existence of the Kingdom of Kush, and its historical roots in the ancient Near East and northeastern Africa can be traced back to periods well before the emergence of Ancient Greece.

- **Kingdom of Kush**: The Kingdom of Kush, as referenced in the Bible with figures like Nimrod, has ancient origins that predate the classical period of Ancient Greece. Nimrod, described as the son of Cush, places the Kingdom of Kush in a timeframe that predates the emergence of Ancient Greece, suggesting an early existence.

- **Ancient Greece:** The classical period of Ancient Greece, marked by city-states like Athens and Sparta, emerged around the 8th century BCE. This is significantly later than the period associated with the Kingdom of Kush and biblical figures like Nimrod.

These revisions reflect the chronological order more accurately, emphasizing that the Kingdom of Kush is mentioned in biblical narratives well before the rise of Ancient Greece.

But is to this region of Kush to which which not only the Christian empires of Alodia and Makuria that we will expound upon in the second

edition, But this is the juncture to establish the source of the Kingdom of Funj of the Kush Sudan region. We're with the greatest of mystery revolves around these empires due to the graphic history and realities of the African warfare and The Royal African War Elephant.

"The Kingdom of Funj and Its Flourishing Legacy with Elephants"

The Kingdom of Funj, situated in what is now Sudan, was a powerful and influential state that thrived from the 15th to the 19th century. While the Funj Kingdom is often celebrated for its strategic location along the Nile River and its contributions to trade, one particularly fascinating aspect of its legacy is its relationship with elephants.

The Funj Kingdom emerged during a period of significant socio-political changes in the Nile Valley. As the Christian Nubian kingdom of Alodia declined, the Funj people, originally from the southern parts of the Nile Valley, established their kingdom with Sennar as its capital. The Funj rulers successfully navigated the challenges of the time and established a powerful and prosperous state.

Trade Routes and Economic Prosperity and the geographical location of the Funj Kingdom was instrumental in its economic prosperity. It served as a hub for trade routes, connecting the African interior to the Red Sea and the Indian Ocean. This strategic position facilitated trade in various commodities, including ivory, gold, spices, and exotic animals.

Elephants held a unique and multifaceted significance within the Funj Kingdom. Symbolically, they were associated with power, royalty, and divine authority. The rulers of the Funj Kingdom recognized the symbolic

importance of elephants and incorporated them into royal ceremonies, further solidifying their role as a symbol of prestige.

Materially, elephants were valuable for their ivory. The Funj Kingdom actively engaged in the ivory trade, exporting this coveted commodity to neighboring regions and beyond. The demand for ivory was high, particularly in the Arab world and parts of Asia, where it was used for various luxury goods and intricate craftsmanship.

The Warfare of Kingdom also harnessed the strength and size of the African Bush Elephants for military purposes. The use of bush elephants in warfare contributed to the military might of the Funj Kingdom, enhancing its ability to defend its territories and expand its influence.

Diplomacy and Elephant Exchanges of The Funj rulers recognized the diplomatic value of elephants. Diplomatic exchanges involving these majestic creatures were not uncommon during this period. Elephants were presented as prestigious gifts to foreign dignitaries, neighboring states, and even distant empires. Such diplomatic gestures were a testament to the wealth and influence of the Funj Kingdom.

Beyond their economic and diplomatic roles, elephants held cultural significance within the Funj Kingdom. Artworks, including sculptures and paintings, depicted elephants as symbols of strength and regality. The cultural representation of elephants further emphasized their importance in the societal fabric of the Funj Kingdom.

The decline of the Funj Kingdom in the 19th century was influenced by various factors, including internal strife, external pressures, and the changing dynamics of trade routes. Despite its eventual decline, the

legacy of the Funj Kingdom, particularly its association with elephants, left an indelible mark on the historical and cultural narrative of the region.

The Kingdom of Funj's relationship with elephants was multifaceted, encompassing economic, diplomatic, military, and cultural dimensions. Elephants played a central role in the kingdom's prosperity, symbolizing both regal authority and material wealth. The legacy of the Funj Kingdom, intertwined with the majestic presence of elephants, remains an intriguing chapter in the history of Sudan and the broader African continent. The detailed dramas of the sultanate must needs take place in the second edition of The Royal African War Elephant in order to begin the unraveling re-emergence of history.

Exert
Evliya Çelebi Travels
-The defeat of Hardigan-

"A King named Hardigan, subordinate to the vuayer of Funjistan. As soon as they saw our soldiers they came down from the hills and headed towards us, a fearless sea-like army of infidels. But our troops stood their ground. When the infidel force, having left the hills and emerged onto the desert, was within range of cannon fire, our monotheist troops let out the cry Allah! Allah! and attacked on their elephants and dromedaries like ants swarming over corpse. The Muslim soldiers attacked from seven directions, the mangonel guns were fired, and the two armies joined the fray. The ensuing battle went on for seven sidercal hours. Y400b Finally, at the time of the afternoon prayer, believing that the Magians had heen routed, the army of Islam found new life and galloped away in pursuit of the fleeing enemy.

On this side, meanwhile, Husayn Bey sent word to the remaining soldiers who came at the time of the evening prayer and halted. 'May your holy war be blessed.' said 1, congratulating Husayn Bey on the victory. This is a favour from God, he replied (citing Qur an 21:23). Rejoicing, he

distributed the booty among the troops. That night he posted sentries to guard the tents, and in the morning he broke camp. He sent the army of Islam to raid and pillage the vilayers of the fire-worshippers, while he himself with another large troop of soldiers halted helow Qal at Firdaniya, from where squadrons set out to ravage the country. All the (enemy's) goods and provisions had been stored in this fortress.

Our commander Husayn Qan entered it with his troops, seized control of all the treasures, and took innumerable captives, whom he clapped in chains. Ordering the soldiery with his heavy baggage to camp. inside the fortress, he himself settled in the palace of Hardigan the fire-worshipper and gave me the palace of Hardiqan's deputy, named Mughan Sir. where I settled in with my retinue.

"Who controls the past controls the future. Who controls the present controls the past?" ~ *George Orwell*

STEFANO DELLA BELLA
(Firenze 1610-1664)

"MOORISH HORSEMAN RIDING TOWARDS RIGHT" c.1651
DESCRIPTION:
A Moorish horseman riding towards left wearing a tiger skin over his shoulders, with a Turkish man standing behind to the left in front of a pyramid, and a caravan traveling towards the right with an elephant.

Chapter 3
Khemite

"When riding on top of an elephant do not assume there is no dew in the thicket."
~ African proverb

The ancient Egyptians referred to their land as "Kemet" or "Kmt," which translates to "the black land." This name likely referred to the fertile black soil along the Nile River, which was crucial for agriculture and provided the foundation for their civilization. The ancient Egyptians also referred to their land as "Ta-Mery," meaning "beloved land" or "land of love."

Herodotus
"The Egyptians were the first to introduce solemn assemblies, processions, and litanies to the gods, also the custom of purifications and festivals, and these were handed on to the Greeks." - Herodotus,

Histories (Book 2.37)
The Word Kmt means Black and the Khemite people call the land " Ta Meri" Happyland. The ancient Khemite/Egyptian word "Netjer,"

which means "god" or "divine" in the ancient Egyptian language. In ancient Egyptian religious beliefs, "Netjer" was used to refer to the deities or divine powers that were worshipped. It encompassed the concept of a higher spiritual presence or cosmic force.

- Neter

-Nature

- Netcher

- Netjeru (plural form)

Notice the similarities of Niger Naga Nagga Negus Negust Negu Negro Nekro.

Similarities of Mery in definitions of Moor.

-Moore

-Blackamoor

-Moor

-Mour

-Muur

-Maur

-Mauri

Netjer: An ancient Egyptian term for "god" or "divine."

Niger: A Latin word meaning "black."

Naga: In various cultures, it can refer to a serpent or snake, and in some contexts, it's associated with mystical or divine significance.

Negus: A title used in Ethiopia and Eritrea, historically referring to a ruler or kind.

Negro: A Spanish term used historically to describe people of African descent,

Nekro: A variant of the Greek word "necro," which is related to death or corpses.

Negrito: A term used to describe various ethnic groups in Southeast Asia, particularly those with small stature and dark skin.

Moore: A surname of English, Irish, or Scottish origin. It may also refer to a person who lived near a moor (a type of landscape dominated by low-growing vegetation) or who worked on one.

Blackamoor: An archaic term used historically to describe a person

with dark skin, often with negative or derogatory connotations. It is now considered offensive and inappropriate.

Moor: Refers to an open area of land, typically covered with heather, grass, and low-growing vegetation. It can also refer to a member of a North African Muslim people, historically inhabiting parts of Spain and Portugal.

Mour: This term could refer to mourning or expressing grief over someone's death.

Muur: This term might be a variant of "Moor" or could be used in a different context.

Maur: A shortened form of "Mauritius," which refers to the island nation in the Indian Ocean.

Mauri: An ancient term used by the Romans to refer to the Berber people of North Africa.

Khemite Mizraim is the Semitic surviving pronounced name of what is now called Egypt. The name Egypt comes from the Greek Aegyptos, which was the greek pronunciation of the Egyptian name 'Hwt-Ka-Ptah,' (meaning "House of the Spirit of Ptah", who was a very early God of the Ancient Egyptians. Khem is the ancestor and founder of what is called Egypt today was and is still called Khemit is the root word for the science of chemistry (Chem). χημία", which is derived from the ancient Egyptian name of Egypt, khem or khm, khame, or khmi, meaning "blackness".

The Khemitic language traces its roots to antiquity, with Old Khemitic emerging around 2690 BCE. Notably, the hieroglyphs featuring elephants are emblematic of Middle Khemitic, a linguistic phase that gained prominence around 2000 BCE. As Khemit evolved, distinct scripts, such as hieroglyphs, hieratic, and demotic, came into use during different epochs of Khemitic history. These scripts served as integral means of communication, inscribed on monumental structures, papyri, and various artifacts. The linguistic tapestry of Khemitic civilization is a testament to its enduring cultural legacy, spanning millennia and captivating scholars and enthusiasts alike with its rich and intricate expressions.

The term "Medu Neter" refers to the ancient Egyptian writing system, commonly known as hieroglyphs. "Medu" translates to "words" or "speech," as we stated before "Neter" means "divine" or "godly." Therefore, Medu Neter can be understood as "divine words" or "divine language."

In ancient Egypt, hieroglyphs were not just a means of communication; they were considered sacred and held a spiritual significance. The writing system was believed to have divine origins and was often associated with Thoth, the god of wisdom, writing, and magic.

The connection of Medu Neter extends beyond mere communication; it played a crucial role in religious texts, monumental inscriptions, and funerary practices. The intricate symbols and characters were used to convey not only mundane information but also religious and spiritual concepts, emphasizing the intertwined nature of language, spirituality, and daily life in ancient Egyptian culture.

African Scene Detail of relief carved by Karl Haberstumpf (1656-1724) and son - detail of a cabinet of wood, made for Emperor Charles VI of the Holy Empire in 1723 at Eger, Czech Republic - (African scene)

Narmer (Ancient Egyptian: n7r-mr, meaning "painful catfish," "stinging catfish," "harsh catfish," or "fierce catfish;" (reign beginning at a date estimated to fall in the range 3273–2987 BC) was an ancient Egyptian pharaoh of the Early Dynastic Period. He was the successor to the Protodynastic king Ka. Many scholars consider him the unifier of Egypt and founder of the First Dynasty, and in turn the first king of a unified Egypt. He also had a prominently noticeable presence in Canaan, compared to his

predecessors and successors. A majority of Egyptologists believe that Narmer was the same person as Menes. Neithhotep is thought to be his queen consort or his daughter. In reading these names and words in their definitions, it is always best to understand what the words mean as a concept when reading and the periodic glimpses into the ancient world will manifest clearly in your understanding and reasoning of the onslaught of psychological settle campaigns waged against the mines and inheritance of people from the present land and the respect for the ancestral dead. As previously mentioned in the second chapter, we established that Kings, leaders and people through rituals or ceremonies change their names or have their names changed relative to events or circumstances.

But in a more defined sense of circumstance of a people finding and or warring for independence and obtaining it, the events, lessons and principles learned through overcoming and defending against the future possibilities of recurrences often renamed places and people related to events once independence was established to do so. An illustration of this would be called a blotting out of one's name from history, and being given a new name unrelated but determined specifically institutionally by a sovereign group of people. Meaning that a story of triumph over a king with a specific name would be renamed in his defeat by the victors. Thus, the future would be determined by the projective wheel of a people's sovereignty in establishing their historical values and cultures distinct from the former oppressor or ruling kingdom.

We also previously mentioned that Nimrod and Narmer are believed by some to be the same person just as Namer and Menes.

*In 450 **BCE the Greek historian Herodotus was taught** 11, 000 years of African history and 300 **Kings, Egypt and Ethiopia***

Book II

"Thus far went the record given me by the Egyptians and their priests; and they showed me that the time from the first king to that priest of Hephaestus, who was the last, covered three hundred and forty one generations of men, and that in this time such also had been the number of their kings, and of their high priests. Now three hundred generations make up ten thousand years, three generations being equal to a century. And over and above the three hundred the remaining forty one cover thirteen hundred and forty years. Thus the whole sum is eleven thousand three hundred and forty years; in all which time (they said) they had had no king who was a god in human farm, nor had there been any such thing either before or after those years among the rest of the kings of Egypt. Tour times in this period (so they told me) the sun rose contrary to his wont; twice he rose where he now sets, and twice he set where now he rises; yet Egypt at these times underwent no change, neither in the produce of the river and the land, nor in the matter of sickness and death."

143 H & WHecataeus19 the historian was once at Thebes, where he made for himself a genealogy which connected him by lineage with a god in the sixteenth p451 generation. But the priests did for him what they did for me (who had not traced my own lineage). They brought me into the great inner court of the temple and showed me there wooden figures which they counted up to the number they had

already given, for every high priest sets there in his lifetime a statue of himself; counting and pointing to these, the priests showed me that each inherited from his father; they went through the whole tale of figures, back to the earliest from that of him who had lateliest died. Thus when Hecataeus had traced his descent and claimed that his sixteenth forefather was a god, the priests too traced a line of descent according to the method of their counting; for they would not be persuaded by him that a man could be descended from a god; they traced descent through the whole line of three hundred and forty-five figures, not connecting it with any ancestral god or hero, but declaring each figure to be a "Piromis" the son of a "Piromis," that is, in the Greek language, one who is in all respects a good man.

Jews of Sudan and the Jewish Temple *in Africa* at Elephantine

The Elephantine Papyri: One of the Most Ancient Collections of
Jewish Manuscripts
Circa 450 BCE
Permalink
Elephantine Temple reconstruction request

"A letter from the Elephantine Papyri, a collection of 5th century BCE writings of the Jewish community at Elephantine in Egypt. Authors are Yedoniah and his colleagues the priests and it is addressed to Bagoas, governor of Judah. The letter is a request for the rebuilding of a Jewish temple at Elephantine, which had been destroyed by Egyptian pagans. The letter is dated year 17 of king

Darius (II) under the rule of the satrap of Egypt, Arsames, which corresponds to 407 BCE."

One of the oldest collections of Jewish manuscripts, dating from the fifth century BCE, the Elephantine papyri were written by the Jewish community at Elephantine (Arabic: جزيرة الفنتين, Greek: Ελεφαντίνη) , then called Yeb, an island in the Nile at the border of NubiaOffsite Link. The Jewish settlement of Elephantine was probably founded as a military installation about 650 BCE, during the reign of Manasseh of Judah, to assist Pharoah Psammetichus IOffsite Link in his Nubian campaign. The dry soil of Upper Egypt preserved documents from the Egyptian border fortresses of Elephantine and Syene . Hundreds of these Elephantine papyri survived, written in hieraticOffsite Link and DemoticOffsite Link Egyptian, Aramaic, Greek, Latin and Coptic, and consisting of legal documents and letters, spanning a period of 1000 years.

"The exact excerpt from the Elephantine Papyri is as follows: *"Now our forefathers built this temple in the fortress of Elephantine in the days of the kingdom of Egypt, and when Cambyses came to Egypt he found this temple built. And they knocked down all the temples of the gods of Egypt, but no one did any damage to this temple. And Cambyses commanded to destroy all the temples of the gods of Egypt, but no one did any damage to this temple. And there were with us as priests Yedoniah and his brothers the priests of the gods. And we went to our lord Bagohi and we said to him*:

Let us rebuild our temple. But he did not do so until the time of Darius king of Egypt. And then our lord Bagohi wrote to Kaiphi the son of Gedaliah and to our lord Delaiah the son of Sanballat and to his colleagues the Apharsachites who lived in Samaria, and they wrote to him to rebuild the temple of Yaho."

"Though some fragments on papyrusOffsite Link are much older, the largest number of papyri are written in AramaicOffsite Link, the lingua franca of the Persian Empire, and document the Jewish community among soldiers stationed at Elephantine under Persian rule, 495-399 BCE. The Elephantine documents include letters and legal contracts from family and other archives: divorce documents, the manumission of slaves, and other business, and are a valuable source of knowledge about law, society, religion, language and onomasticsOffsite Link, the sometimes surprisingly revealing study of names...." (Wikipedia article on Elephantine papyri, accessed 12-09-2013).

Porten, Bezalel et al, The Elephantine Papyri in English. Three Millennia of Cross-Cultural Continuity

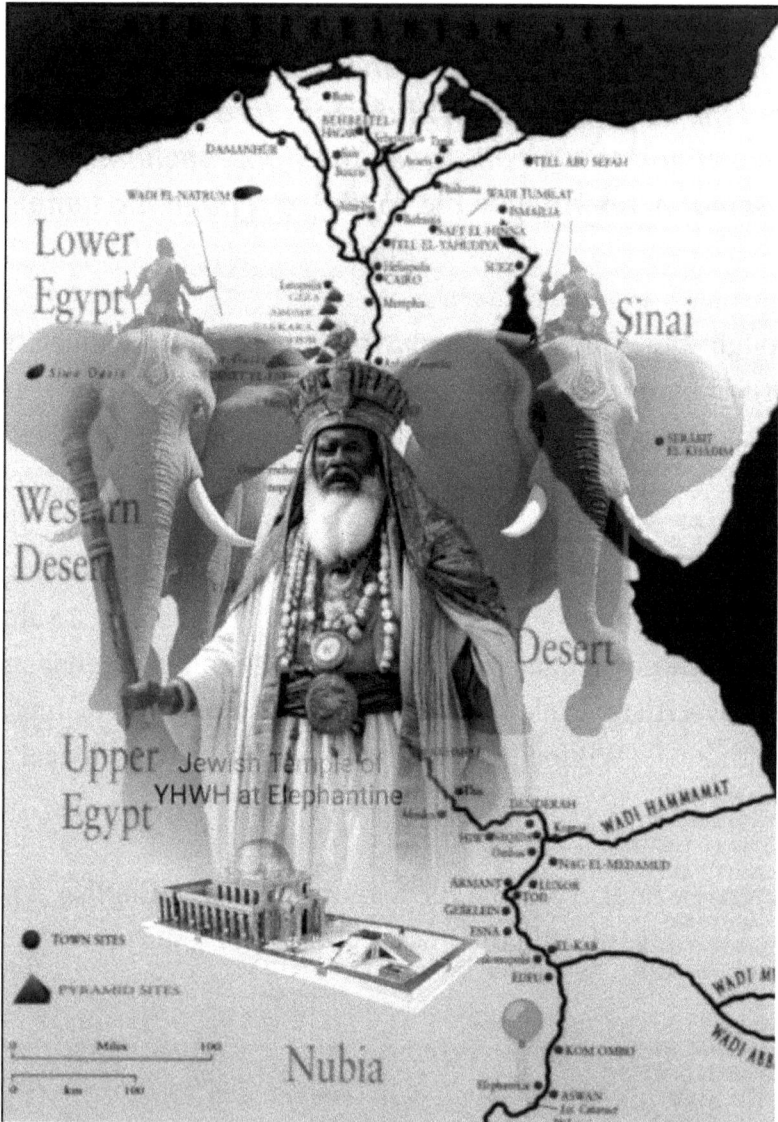

The ancient island in the Nile River near modern-day Aswan in Egypt, holds a significant place in history as a center for the trade of tame African elephants and other exotic animals. At the heart of

this bustling trade hub was the Jewish community who played a crucial role in the religious and commercial activities of the region.

The island of Elephantine served as a strategic location for trade between Egypt and its southern territories, including Nubia and further south into Africa. One of the most notable commodities traded was the African elephant, prized for its strength, intelligence, and versatility. These magnificent creatures were used for various purposes, including transportation, labor, and even warfare.

The Jewish community of Elephantine, believed to have been established in the 7th century BCE, lived alongside other ethnic groups in the region. They worshipped Yahweh, the God of Israel, and built a temple dedicated to him on the island. This temple served as a spiritual center for the Jewish inhabitants, who continued their religious practices despite being far from their homeland.

The Jews of Elephantine were not only religious practitioners but also active participants in the commercial affairs of the island. They engaged in trade, including the export of exotic animals like elephants, which were in high demand across the ancient world. Through their connections and expertise, they facilitated the transportation and sale of these valuable commodities to various destinations, contributing to the prosperity of the region.

The trade of tame elephants was a lucrative business, attracting merchants and traders from far and wide. Elephants were highly

prized by rulers, military commanders, and wealthy individuals who sought to showcase their power and status through ownership of these majestic animals. The Jews of Elephantine played a central role in this trade network, leveraging their knowledge of the local terrain and their relationships with indigenous peoples to acquire and transport elephants safely and efficiently.

Elephant taming was a specialized skill mastered by the inhabitants of Elephantine and neighboring regions. Taming these wild creatures required patience, courage, and intimate knowledge of elephant behavior. The process involved capturing young elephants, known as calves, and training them to obey commands and perform various tasks. Skilled trainers, known as mahouts, formed close bonds with their elephants, forging relationships based on trust and mutual respect.

The presence of tame elephants on Elephantine not only fueled the exotic animal trade but also contributed to the island's cultural and social fabric. Elephants were featured in religious ceremonies, public events, and artistic expressions, symbolizing strength, wisdom, and divine favor. Their majestic presence captivated the imaginations of residents and visitors alike, leaving an indelible mark on the island's history and identity.

In conclusion, Elephantine emerged as a vibrant center for the trade of tame African elephants and other exotic animals, driven by the ingenuity and enterprise of its diverse inhabitants, including the Jewish community. Through their religious devotion, commercial

acumen, and cultural contributions, the Jews of Elephantine played a pivotal role in shaping the island's destiny and leaving a lasting legacy in the annals of history. In addition to the Jewish community, Meroetic Cushite merchants were integral to the bustling trade hub of Elephantine. The Meroitic Kingdom, centered around the city of Meroe in present-day Sudan, was a major economic and political power in the region, known for its wealth, cultural sophistication, and strategic location along the Nile River.

Meroitic Cushite merchants were renowned for their expertise in long-distance trade, particularly in luxury goods such as gold, ivory, incense, and exotic animals. They established extensive trade networks that extended across the Red Sea into Arabia, down the Nile into Egypt, and westward into North Africa. These merchants played a crucial role in connecting the Mediterranean world with the riches of Africa, contributing to the prosperity and prestige of their kingdom.

The Meroitic Cushites were adept at navigating the complex political landscape of the ancient Near East, forging diplomatic alliances and commercial partnerships with neighboring kingdoms and empires. They maintained cordial relations with the Jewish community of Elephantine, engaging in mutually beneficial trade and cultural exchange. The presence of Meroitic Cushite merchants added to the cosmopolitan character of Elephantine, enriching its cultural diversity and economic vitality.

Among the prominent figures in the Jewish community of Elephantine were the high priests and leaders who presided over the religious and communal affairs of the island. These individuals played key roles in maintaining the integrity of the Jewish faith, administering the temple rituals, and representing the community in matters of governance and diplomacy.

One of the most notable high priests mentioned in the Elephantine papyri is Jedaniah, who served during the Persian period in the 5th century BCE. Jedaniah is mentioned in several documents, including letters addressed to him and references to his role in temple administration. He was responsible for overseeing the religious activities of the temple, including sacrifices, offerings, and festivals, and ensuring the adherence of the community to Jewish law and tradition.

Other prominent Jewish leaders mentioned in the Elephantine papyri include Bagohi, who served as the governor of Judah under the Persian administration, and Delaiah and Shelemiah, who were officials in the Jewish community of Elephantine. These individuals played important roles in negotiating with local authorities, managing communal resources, and representing the interests of the Jewish population.

The Jewish high priests and leaders of Elephantine were tasked with navigating the complex political and social dynamics of the region, balancing the demands of Persian rule with the religious and cultural identity of the Jewish community. They upheld the sanctity

of the temple and the integrity of Jewish worship while also fostering peaceful coexistence with their neighbors and facilitating economic prosperity through trade and diplomacy.

In conclusion, the Jewish community of Elephantine flourished as a vibrant center of religious devotion, commercial enterprise, and cultural exchange, thanks in part to the contributions of Meroitic Cushite merchants and the leadership of Jewish high priests and leaders. Through their collective efforts, they helped shape the destiny of the island and left a lasting legacy that continues to resonate in the annals of history.

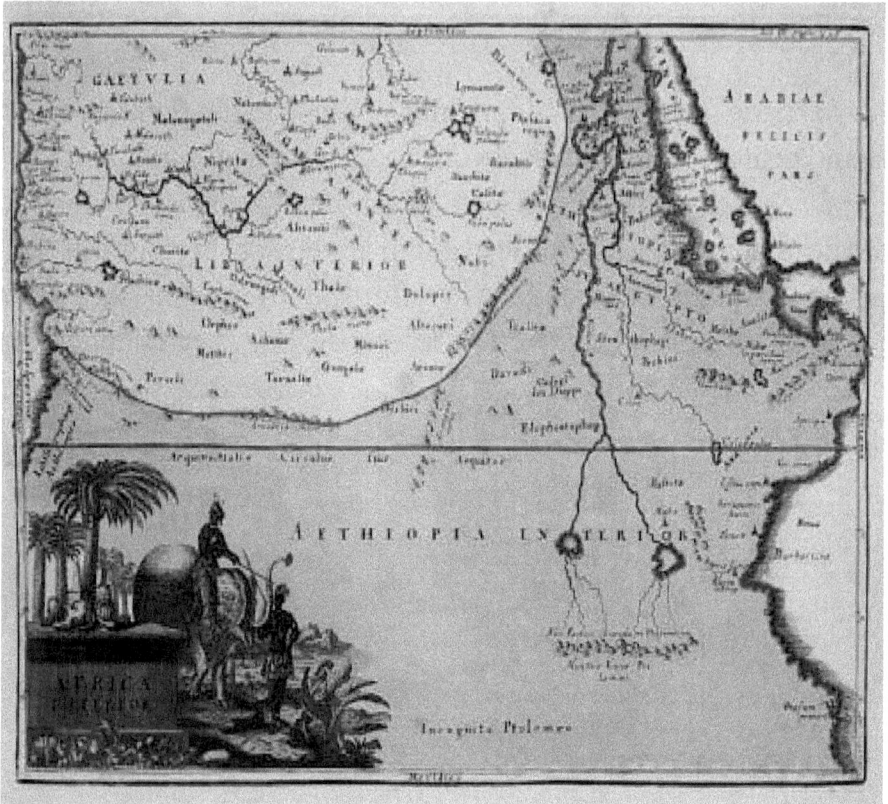

c. 3200–3000 BC; /ˈmeɪneɪz/; Ancient Egyptian: mnj, probably

pronounced */maˈnij/;Ancient Greek: Μήνης) was a pharaoh of the
Early Dynastic Period of ancient Egypt credited by classical
tradition with having united Upper and Lower Egypt and as the
founder of the First Dynasty.

The prominent Ancient True Khemite first leaders of accepted Khemite History.

Narmer (c. 3100 BC) - Unified Upper and Lower Egypt.

Djoser (c. 2670 BC) - Constructed the Step Pyramid.

Sneferu (c. 2613–2589 BC) - Constructed the Bent Pyramid and Red Pyramid.

Khufu (c. 2589–2566 BC) - Built the Great Pyramid of Giza.

Hatshepsut (c. 1478–1458 BC) - One of the few female pharaohs.

Thutmose III (c. 1479–1425 BC) - Known for military campaigns.

Amenhotep III (c. 1386–1349 BC) - Oversaw a period of prosperity.

Akhenaten (c. 1353–1336 BC) - Introduced the Aten cult.

Tutankhamun (c. 1332–1323 BC) - Famous for his intact tomb.

Ramses II (c. 1279–1213 BC) - Engaged in battles and construction projects.

Ramses III (c. 1186–1155 BC) - Fought off invasions and built monuments.

The Ancient Khemites ships sailed the Mediterranean for trade purposes, their trade network extended towards the Mediterranean and Red Seas. The use of war elephants as prehistoric reality is common sense as the main trade partners of ancient Khemite Egypt were regions around the Mediterranean, such as the Levant and Kush Nubia, and their trade extended to the Arabian Peninsula, East Africa, and other parts of the ancient world.

Now here is where it all comes together: in the origin and the necessity for one's mind to perceive the ancient world coming together is as we said before, the world is upside down. In viewing a world map or an actual South top map that has now reoccurred due to people's desire to restore proper perspective in reading historical narratives and accounts that differ from culture to culture, but the principles remain the same at the same time observing the geography to which people moved and how climates play a role, especially in the southern hemisphere relative to Rome's inability to pierce Africa and Alexander the great's inability to pierce India. You can see and understand that the world of the Mediterranean in ancient times, especially and Even prophetically Jerusalem and the

Dead Sea being the lowest place on earth is obvious. Even though Egypt had built a great civilization and sailed the high seas of the Mediterranean, the Sea of reeds which is called the see if Kush as we will show also, what is now called the Atlantic Ocean was known as the Ethiopian ocean.

Africa
2450 B.C
Crossing The Red Sea (colour litho) by French School, (19th century); Private Collection; (add.info.: Crossing The Red Sea. Illustration for Histoire Sainte (Guerin, c 1890). Illustrations by " H Grobet".);

The first Hebrew tabernacle, often referred to as the Tabernacle of Moses or the Tent of Meeting, was erected in the Sinai Peninsula, which is located in the northeastern part of the African continent. The account of the construction and use of the Tabernacle is described in the biblical books of Exodus, Leviticus, and Numbers.

The Israelites, led by Moses, constructed the Tabernacle during their wanderings in the wilderness after the Exodus from Egypt. The biblical narrative places the Tabernacle in the desert regions around Mount Sinai. The exact location is not precisely identified, but it is generally associated with the Sinai Peninsula in northeastern Africa. And to properly refer to the land as it was called in that day .. the land of Khem/ Khemet before Greece and existed.

(Herodotus book 2)

100

Rawlinson p164

"After him came three hundred and thirty kings, whose names the priests recited from a papyrus roll. In all these many generations there were eighteen Ethiopian kings, and one queen, native to the country; the rest were all Egyptian men. The name of the queen was the same as that of the Babylonian princess, Nitocris. She, to avenge her brother (he was king of Egypt and was slain by his subjects, who then gave Nitocris sovereignty) put

p389

many of the Egyptians to death by guile. She built a spacious underground chamber; then, with the pretence of handselling it, but

135

with far other intent in her mind, she gave a great feast, inviting to it those Egyptians whom she knew to have been most concerned in her brother's murder; and while they feasted she let the river in upon them

by a great and secret channel. This was all that the priests told of her, save that also when she had done this she cast herself into a chamber full of hot ashes, thereby to escape vengeance.

101
Rawlinson p166

But of the other kings, they related no achievement or deed of great note, save of Moeris, who was the last of them. This Moeris was remembered as having built the northern forecourt of the temple of Hephaestus, dug a lake, of as many furlongs in a circuit as I shall later show; and built their pyramids also, the size of which I will mention when I speak of the lake. All this was Moeris' work, they said; none of the rest had anything to record.

102
H & W

Passing over these, therefore, I will now speak of the king who came after them, Sesostris.1 This king, said the priests, set out with a fleet of long ships2 from the Arabian Gulf and subdued all the dwellers by the Red Sea, till as he sailed on he came to a sea which was too shallow for his vessels. After returning thence back to Egypt, he gathered a great army (according to the story of the priests) and marched over the mainland, subduing every nation to

p391

which he came. When those that he met were valiant men and strove
army and left it there to dwell in the country, or it may be that some of his soldiers grew weary of his wanderings, and stayed by the Phasis.

For it is plain to see that Colchians are Egyptians; and this that I say I noted before I heard it from others. When I hard for freedom, he set up pillars in their land whereon the inscription showed his name and his country's, and how he had overcome them with his power; but when the cities had made no resistance and been easily taken, then he put an inscription on the pillars even as he had done where the nations were brave; but he drew also on them the privy parts of a woman, wishing to show clearly that the people were cowardly" doing he marched over the country till he had passed over from Asia to Europe and subdued the Scythians and Thracians. Thus far and no farther, I think, the Egyptian army went; for the pillars can be seen standing in their country, but in none beyond it.

Thence he turned about and went back homewards; and when he came to the Phasis river, it may be (for I cannot speak with exact knowledge) that King Sesostris divided off some part of hisbegan to think on this matter, I inquired of both peoples; and the Colchians remembered the Egyptians better than the Egyptians remembered the Colchians; the Egyptians said that they held the Colchians to be part of Sesostris' army. I myself guessed it to be p393 so, partly because they are dark-skinned and woolly-haired; though that indeed goes for nothing, seeing that other peoples, too, are such; but

my better proof was that the Colchians and Egyptians and Ethiopians are the only nations that have from the first practised circumcision.

The Phoenicians and the Syrians of Palestine acknowledge of themselves that they learnt the custom from the Egyptians, and the Syrians of the valleys of the Thermodon and the Parthenius, as well as their neighbours the Macrones, say that they learnt it lately from the Colchians. These are the only nations that circumcise, and it is seen that they do even as the Egyptians. But as to the Egyptians and Ethiopians themselves, I cannot say which nation learnt it from the other; for it is manifestly a very ancient custom. That the others learnt it from intercourse with Egypt I hold to be proved by this — that Phoenicians who hold intercourse with Hellas cease to imitate the Egyptians in this matter and do not circumcise their children

Rawlinson p172Nay, and let me speak of another matter in which the Colchians are like to the Egyptians; they and the Egyptians alone work linen, and have the same way, a way peculiar to themselves, of working it; and they are alike in all their manner of life, and in their speech. Linen has two names: the Colchian kind is called by the Greeks Sardinian;3 that which comes from Egypt is called Egyptian."

This excerpt from Herodotus book 2 is in regards to the Egyptian pharaohs and the statements of the hair type and skin color of the Egyptians as well as the Ethiopians.

Africa
" Africa from a set of The Four Continents - tapestry by Jean Jacques François Le Barbier" (1738-1826)
African Egyptians and mounted elephant pyramid in background.

To recount our steps as we have come this far, pleasEdynasties of Khemite Mizraim and having taken control of Kemet, Egypt for several dynasties being known as the Golden Dynasties these

empires have shared trade goods, technology, ancestries and cultures and all having traded ivory, elephants, gold, animal skins.

Ancient Egyptian Kemite warriors wielded an array of formidable weapons and donned impressive armor. Their primary weapons included the khopesh, a curved sword, and the composite bow. The khopesh's unique shape enabled slashing and stabbing motions, while the composite bow ensured long-range accuracy. The warriors' armor consisted of bronze or leather cuirasses, providing vital protection. In grand battles, they employed elephant tactics by strategically deploying these colossal beasts as living battering rams, trampling adversaries and causing chaos. Similarly, ancient Nubian Kushite fighters wielded spears, axes, and shields made of animal skins, embracing a lightweight yet sturdy approach. They also utilized elephants, utilizing their size and strength to disrupt enemy formations and inspire fear on the battlefield.

Search

"An Egyptian mural from the Rekhmire Tomb (c. 1479 to 1401 BCE during the XVIII dynasty) shows what appears to be a baby mammoth. The artist portrayed an elephant-like creature with lots of hair, a convex back, a high-domed head, and tusks. "

Quotes from Diodorus Siculus that highlight the achievements and mastery of the ancient Egyptians:

"They alone, the Egyptians, hold the opinion that learning is a necessary possession, not for the sake of any external application, but to become acquainted with the most secret matters, and, as it were, to pry into the very nature of things." - Diodorus Siculus, *Library of History* (Book 1.81.3)

"The Egyptians are said to have been the first to teach the science

of geometry." - Diodorus Siculus, *Library of History* (Book 1.96.1)

Four Continents: Africa

Antonio Zucchi, RA (Venice 1726 - Rome 1796)

"The Egyptians, who have always devoted themselves to education and instruction, surpass all other nations in the accuracy of their knowledge." - Diodorus Siculus, *Library of History* (Book 1.79.3)

"The Egyptians are considered to be superior to all other nations in almost all forms of wisdom and learning." - Diodorus Siculus, *Library of History* (Book 1.21.2)

"The Egyptians have paid much attention to the study of geometry and mechanics." - Diodorus Siculus, *Library of History* (Book 1.59.1)

So it is evident to note that we have clarity of the taming and mastering and development of wildlife and breeding of giraffes, elephants and the rhinoceros as well as the hippopotamus all animals of the region which for some is hard to understand. But this is Africa, the ancient world and a world without time which strikes at the core instinct and soul of Man. Although in this summary of Egyptian history, it has become common knowledge that the ancient civilization and people of Nubia Kush Meroe are in reality the same family branch of civilization that Egypt later became distinct and separate, developing its identity to the Down North.

The debate and war of names is a war of culture and association. The association of current people who live in North Africa who identify as Arabs identify themselves as Egyptian and rightfully so because they are the defenders of the land. However, that does not mean the civilization predated those who did not identify as Arabs in their native tribes and the names of their ancestors and the names of their principles and sciences that even the European explorers such as Heroditis the author of this history distinguished them of Kemet to be the same people to the south and did not identify as nomad Arabs although the ancient Arab in the land was that of melanated Semitic and Kushitic ancestries as well, though having themselves become distinct in the creations of cultures and ancestral identities.

The book 3 Maccabees 5
Two angels save the Jews from Ptolemy IV Philopator's drunken
elephants, by Jan Luyken, 1700.

The book of Jasher, an ancient Hebrew text mentioned in the Bible
(Joshua 10:13, 2 Samuel 1:18), provides additional details about the

relationship between Abraham's son Ishmael and his Egyptian mother. According to Jasher 16:10-11, after Sarah gave Hagar, an Egyptian, to Abraham as a wife, they dwelled in Egypt for a while. During this time, Pharaoh's daughter, Bityah, took Hagar into her household and raised Ishmael as her own.

Regarding the Ishmaelites being involved in slave trading, the Bible does mention their association with the slave trade. In Genesis 37:25-28, when Joseph was sold into slavery by his brothers, a group of Ishmaelites is described as passing by, carrying spices, balm, and myrrh, on their way to Egypt. Later, it is revealed that they sold Joseph to Potiphar, an Egyptian officer.

While the Ishmaelites' involvement in the slave trade is briefly mentioned in the Bible, the specific connection to their Egyptian ancestry through Hagar is explicitly stated as She is their grandmother. The narrative primarily focuses on the descendants of Ishmael becoming a great nation and dwelling in the wilderness (Genesis 21:13-21). The Book of Jasher offers additional details about Ishmael's upbringing and his connection to Khemite Egypt through his mother's relationship with Pharaoh's daughter.

Hagar, the Khemite, occupies a pivotal place in the annals of history as the mother of Ishmael and an emblem of Khemitic African ancestry. Her legacy is an indelible mark of the intricate connections between Africa and the Arabian Peninsula. Hagar's origins in Khemit (Egypt) speak to an undoubted lineage that can be traced beyond question to the heart of Africa.

As the mother of Ishmael, Hagar's African ancestry indubitably flowed through her veins, imprinting her son with a heritage that transcended geographical boundaries. The Ishmaelites, descendants of Ishmael, solidified the interplay of African lineages in Arabian history. Their marriages to Africans are undisputedly recorded as an aspect of their legacy, marking an unarguable testament to the intermingling of cultures and ancestries.

Hagar's journey, marked by her role in the lineage of Abraham and the birth of Ishmael, is a crystal-clear illustration of the rich tapestry of human migration and interaction. Her African ancestry, beyond a shadow of a doubt, is a thread that weaves through the intricate narratives of Arabian history, leaving an indomitable mark on the story of Ishmael and the Ishmaelites.

Incontestably, Hagar's presence in the lineage of Ishmael and the Ishmaelites signifies the enduring connections between Africa and Arabia. Her story echoes with the certainty that goes without saying of shared lineages and cultural exchanges that shaped the identities of people across borders and continents. Hagar, the Khemite, and her descendants, the Ishmaelites, stand as living testaments to the undeniable and crystal-clear presence of African ancestry in the tapestry of Khemitic Arabian history. The trade relationship between the early Hebrew civilizations, ancient

Axumite Empire and the Kingdom of Kush were a vital economic and cultural exchange that spanned across the Reed Sea and a land border. Historical sources substantiate the importance of this trade

route, particularly for the exchange of precious commodities like ivory and gold.

Ancient texts and archaeological evidence confirm the thriving ivory trade between Axum and Kush. The ivory obtained from the African elephants of Kush was highly sought after by the Axumites, who used it for intricate carvings and crafts. Additionally, the Kingdom of Kush's rich gold mines supplied Axum with precious metals, fueling its economy and further strengthening its bond.

The trade connections between Hebrew, Axum, Kush, and the Egyptians also flourished along the Nile. The Kushite Empire, known for its wealth and power, traded not only gold and ivory with the Egyptians but also exotic animals like elephants and giraffes. These valuable resources served as symbols of prestige and contributed to the cultural exchanges between the empires.

Furthermore, the enduring impact of these trade networks is evident in the DNA makeup of modern populations. Genetic studies have revealed genetic connections and shared ancestry between peoples of ancient Axum, Kush, and Egypt. This attests to the long-standing interactions and intermingling of ethnic groups facilitated by these trade routes. And the three main types of scripts and languages but only two were used in trade:

Hieroglyphs: This is the most well-known script, consisting of pictorial symbols. It was used for monumental inscriptions, religious texts, and important documents. Hieroglyphs were used as early as the

Predynastic period, around 3300 BCE. Making the hieroglyphs nearly 6,000 years old.

Hieratic: Hieratic script was a cursive form of hieroglyphs used for everyday writing, administrative documents, and religious texts. It was faster to write than hieroglyphs. It emerged around the same time as hieroglyphs and continued to be used for several thousand years.

Demotic: Demotic script developed later and was used for various purposes, including legal and administrative documents, as well as literature. It's considered the "everyday" script of ancient Egypt. Demotic script emerged around 660 BCE and continued to be used until the 5th century CE.

These scripts were used to write the Egyptian language, which evolved and had several stages including Old Egyptian,

The Four Continents: Africa
Antonio Zucchi (1726-1796) National Trust, Kedleston Hall and
Eastern Museum

Middle Egyptian, Late Egyptian, and more. For trade and administrative purposes, the ancient Egyptians primarily used the "hieratic" script. Hieratic was a cursive script derived from hieroglyphs, but it was much faster to write. It was well-suited for day-to-day activities such as record-keeping, correspondence, and trade documentation. Hieratic was more practical than the elaborate hieroglyphs, which were often reserved for monumental

inscriptions, religious texts, and other special purposes. And amazingly, the Arabic script looks extremely similar. To which we will touch on in the next coming chapters.

In conclusion, the trade routes connecting the Axumite Empire, the Kingdom of Kush, and the Egyptians were pivotal in shaping the economies, cultures, and genetic makeup of these ancient civilizations. The exchange of ivory, gold, and exotic animals fostered prosperity and cultural enrichment, leaving an indelible mark on the history and heritage of the regions involved.

Search
"Dendera temple: hieroglyphs in Khemite Mizraim" Elephant with mounted rider

The ancient Kemetic word " mnd"

Aa, Pieter van der, 1659-1733

Nigritie, ou le pays des Negres en Afrique, avec tous ses royaumes, bayes, rivières et ports de mer, suivant les meilleures relations de ceux qui ont été sur les lieux, et nouvellement mise au jour.
[graphic] / par Pierre Vander AA.
Title
Nigritie, or the countries of the blacks in Africa.
Publisher

A Leide: Marchand Libraire Date
[1729?]

TOTIUS AFRICAE ACCURATISSIMA TABULA AUTHORE
FREDERICO DE WIT
Frederick de Wit (*1630 - †1706)
Coloured map of the African continent. Printed in Amsterdam circa
1680.

Chapter 4
Phoenicians, Moors, And Kanem Barnu

"Until the lion learns to speak, the tale of the hunt will always glorify the hunter." - African Proverb

"**Jugurtha (circa 160–104 BC)** - Jugurtha was a Numidian king who is known for his involvement in the Jugurthine War, a conflict against Rome. He employed War Elephants in his military efforts against the Romans and their allies."

Jugurtha, a historical figure dating back to around 160–104 BC, was a significant Numidian king whose legacy is intertwined with the indigenous black African people of North Africa. His reign and involvement in the Jugurthine War provide us with insights into the complex interplay of ethnicity, geography, and power dynamics during this ancient period.

Jugurtha hailed from the Kingdom of Numidia, a region located in what is now modern-day Algeria and Tunisia. The Numidians were an indigenous North African people with a rich cultural and historical heritage. Ethnically, they were part of the larger Berber ethnic group, known for their deep connection to the land and their diverse languages and traditions. The Numidians were adept at

utilizing the resources of their land, including the indigenous African elephants that inhabited the region.

The Kingdom of Numidia held a strategic position in North Africa, making it a significant player in regional politics and conflicts. Jugurtha's lineage is traced back to the ruling elites of Numidia, and he inherited both the strengths and complexities of his Numidian heritage. As an indigenous black African leader, Jugurtha's rule was marked by his efforts to maintain the sovereignty of his kingdom against external powers, particularly Rome.

"History of Scipio Africanus Battle of Zama"
Africa

Jugurtha's involvement in the Jugurthine War against Rome showcased his determination to protect his kingdom from foreign

influence. In his military campaigns, he employed war elephants, which were tamed and trained by the indigenous people of the region. These indigenous black African people had developed a deep understanding of the land and its inhabitants, including the elephants. Through their expertise, they were able to harness the strength and abilities of these majestic creatures for military purposes.

The indigenous black African ancestry of the people who tamed and trained the war elephants underscores their intimate connection to the land and the ecosystem. Their knowledge of the environment, the behaviour of the elephants, and the intricate dynamics of warfare in the region gave them a unique advantage. This expertise was passed down through generations, creating a legacy of skillful elephant handlers who contributed to the military strategies of leaders like Jugurtha.

The tribes associated with the indigenous black African people who trained and tamed the elephants have evolved. While the specific ancient tribes might not have direct modern counterparts, the Berber ethnic group, of which the Numidians were a part, still exists in the region. Berber languages, collectively known as Amazigh languages, continue to be spoken by various communities across North Africa. These languages, often written using scripts such as Tifinagh, are a testament to the enduring cultural heritage of the indigenous people.

In modern times, various tribes and communities in Algeria, Tunisia, and neighbouring regions are part of the Berber cultural legacy. Tribes like the Kabyles, Tuaregs, and Chleuhs are connected to this heritage and continue to preserve elements of their indigenous identity. While the historical context has evolved, the legacy of the indigenous black African people's expertise in training elephants and their deep connection to the land remains an important aspect of the region's history.

In conclusion, Jugurtha's role as a Numidian king who employed war elephants in the Jugurthine War sheds light on the indigenous black African people's intricate relationship with their environment, their land, and their cultural heritage. The Berber ethnicity, encompassing various tribes and communities, carries forward the legacy of the ancient Numidians and their connection to the indigenous African elephant. The expertise of these indigenous people in training elephants is a testament to their ancestral knowledge and their integral role in shaping the history of North Africa. These Numidian kings played a significant role in the use of war elephants in North Africa during their respective times.

In this segment, it may prove necessary to indicate some observations regarding ethnicities. Seeing that throughout the process of time, it has become a common thing for people in modern times to disassociate themselves by separating the southern Saharan groups of people from the northern families. According to modern terminologies, It's part of him in nature to associate and

disassociate with Ken and with people of relative resemblance. To this matter, let us establish this point. For the most part, it is most likely that are readers who are new to this history. May have never heard of the kingdom of Numidia. Although it is a commonly known Empire for historians and those who study Mediterranean and African history. But it is most common for the average person to be familiar with Hannibal of Carthage because of his entrance into Rome and his illustrious battle of annihilation which we will touch on in if you just segment.

And it is most notable for there to be an issue between identifying the race of Hannibal which we will not identify nor will we suggest any. But it should be understood that in most cases the names mentioned of the warriors and kings that are not very well known, should be understood to be African simply because most likely all identities of these individuals are not mainstream. Furthermore, let us establish this foundation.

When it comes to race in this regard, let us understand and agree that the majority of the world is non-white simply because those of the world are not identified as white by those who identify themselves as white. The majority of human history and civilization is identified by the name of ancestors and nation. To this point let us establish.

Old Genoese world map Atlas 1457 Vintage World Map

In this particular map Africa at the left bottom corner. Although the map is turned sideways, see The Royal African War Elephant with tower in the close-up

Exert

(map) by Jacobo Russo (Giacomo Russo) of Messina (1533)

(North Africa showing War elephant encampments across the continent)

(Web search for high definition resolution)

P.71

"The thing is, it was at first a small city founded by the Africans on the bank of the lake consisting of the La Goulette channel, about a million.

Fearing the advent of a leader from and after the destruction of Carthage, the city of Tunis began to grow, whether in the number of houses or the number of the population. The soldiers who occupied Carthage refused to reside in it. The enemy extended it from Europe, so they settled in Tunisia and built a role there. Then Uthman came before Uthman, the third of the Rightly Guided Caliphs, named Uqba, and he commanded his army. Not to reside in any city located near the sea or on the beach itself. That is why he built the city, which was called Kairouan, thirty-six miles from the sea and one hundred miles from Tunis, so the soldiers left Tunisia and settled in Kairouan, and the people of Tunisia entered the homes that the soldiers had vacated.

After the passage of nearly three hundred and fifty years, the Arabs destroyed Kairouan following the revolution of the governor of Ifriqiya, who was left by the Caliph Al-Qaim, so that this governor fled towards the west and ruled Bejaia and all the surrounding countries (49).

Hassan Hosni Abd al-Wahhab mentioned in his book Waraqat (1:290) that the name of Tunisia is of Phoenician origin (Thunes) and it was mentioned among the villages that existed during the imposition era as two generations, not in the era of the Romans and the Byzantines, but it did not have a large share in the history of the country Until Commander Hassan bin Al-Numan came in the year

69 AH to besiege Cartagena and take the village of Tunis as the base of the camp for him to seize Cartagena a thousand to restore its old greatness and leave it in the hands of taking Tunisia instead, so he built it and built the Zaytuna Mosque in it, and dug a wide bay connecting its lake with the sea from Jahni Rades and the throat the valley. (19) Al-Mu'izz ibn Badis set out for Mahdia in Ramadan 449 November 1957, after he was defeated by the Bedouin of Bani Hilal, reconciled with them, and vacated the Qiran for them. Al-Hassan Al-Wazzan here confuses the two Sanhajit emirates: the eastern Zamara of Kairouan, and the western emirate of Qal'at Hamad. Consideration: Details of that according to Hassan Hosni Abd al-Wahhab, a summary of the history of Tunisia between 109-115"

It is only a group of people who identify themselves that can determine whether or not one is acceptable to that group. For this matter, it is the determination of what was to become the United States of America under the leadership of George Washington that established in the 1790 Nationalization Act that the country was for only those "free white persons". Not Asians not Italians. Not Africans not Middle Easterners. Not Indians not sub-Saharan not East, African or Egyptian. But that the reserved citizenship of the United States was for that of free white persons. As that being the model for anyone entering the shores of that territory, sadly slavery would be the fate of that era. Though not much different from any other nation of that time where ancestry and freedom were hand in hand.

This is mentioned to establish a point that the race of individuals or not factored into the study but to that of the continent of Africa. The African peoples in the endeavors of African civilizations. Although The point of this book is that it is a collection of illustrations and depictions of indigenous African people's and empires taming training and engaging the use of the indigenous African elephant as a beast of burden and war and labor, as this is the focus of this work of restoration and circulation of these depicted illustrations.

The region encompassing North Africa and surrounding areas witnessed the presence of diverse tribal groups. These groups shared common experiences that linked them through their interactions, languages, and cultures:

- **Berbers and Tuareg**:
The Berber people formed a significant presence in North Africa, interacting with various civilizations, including Carthage. Their ancestral roots connect them to the ancient inhabitants of the region. Among the Berber groups, the Tuareg, known for their nomadic lifestyle, maintained their unique identity, influenced by centuries of cross-cultural exchanges.

- **Phoenicians and Carthaginians**: The Phoenicians, who established Carthage, were part of the larger Semitic-speaking family.
While the term "Semitic" refers to linguistic connections, the historical ties between the Phoenicians and other Semitic cultures are evident in their trade networks and shared influences.

P.Aveline In.   P. Aveline sculp.

Vous qu'anime sans cesse un dangereux courroux,   L'AFRIQUE   *Dans les brûlants sablons de ce Pais stérile*
Sanguinaires Lyons, dont l'Afrique est l'azile,   *Les Hommes ne sont pas plus traitables que vous*
                                    a Paris chés Aveline rue St Jacques à la Reine de France.

Africa: landscape with Black man conversing with a woman;
elephant, palm tree, lions and Black men on
Etching and engraving
Print made by: Pierre Aveline
Published by: Pierre Aveline
School/style
French
Production date
1717-1760

- **Kanuri and Lake Chad Region**: The Kanuri people, native to the Lake Chad region, played a pivotal role in the Kanem-Barnu

Empire. This empire's establishment and growth were deeply intertwined with the Kanuri culture and historical developments in the region.

By recognizing these interconnected threads, we gain a richer understanding of the dynamic history of the groups that shaped North Africa and surrounding areas. Their interactions, languages, and cultures of shared experiences, leaving a lasting impact on the region's historical narrative.

The Empire of Kanem Bornu is the empire that goes underneath the radar of so many students of history. Kanem Bornu is perhaps the longest reigning Empire in world history being centred in the Sahara area of what is now known as Chad and Niger Nigeria. The Kanem Empire is one of the world-renowned. Kanem emerged as a powerful kingdom in the ancient region known as the Lake Chad Basin, which is located in present-day Chad and northeastern Nigeria. The empire's origins can be traced back to the 9th century, when a group of Berber-speaking pastoralists, believed to be indigenous North Africans, migrated southward from the areas encompassing modern-day Libya, Egypt, and Kush Sudan. These Berber settlers established the foundation of the Kanem

Empire, blending their cultural practices with the local African populations. They founded dynasties that ruled over the

region for centuries, building a prosperous and formidable kingdom. The empire's strategic location along the Saharan trade routes facilitated its engagement in extensive trade networks, particularly in ivory, slaves, and other valuable commodities.

The Kanem Empire became renowned for its military prowess, employing an extravagant cavalry and even incorporating war elephants into their ranks. These powerful forces allowed them to expand their territories and engage in numerous wars, both defensive and offensive, against neighbouring kingdoms. Their conflicts with various powers, including Libya, Egypt, and Kush Sudan, were often characterised by fierce battles and territorial disputes.

The empire's linguistic landscape was rich and diverse, with a fusion of Berber, Arabic, and local African languages. This linguistic fusion was reflective of the cultural amalgamation that occurred within the empire's borders.

Remarkably, the Kanem Empire endured for centuries, outlasting the mighty Roman Empire. Its economic prosperity, military strength, and cultural diversity contributed to its longevity. However, over time, internal conflicts, external pressures, and the rise of new regional powers eventually led to the decline of the Kanem Empire in the 19th century. Nevertheless, its legacy as a significant force in the history of West Africa endures, and its story is one of a dynamic and influential empire that shaped the region for centuries.

Africa, Martin Engelbrecht, German, 1684–1756, C.F. Lottes, 1701 - 1740, Engraving on paper, Scene representing Africa. Woman seated on an elephant under a palm tree, holding a parasol. A man offering her a plate of nuts., Germany, Augsburg, Germany, 1717, Print

Now after having established and connected principles of empires along the Nile and the geography of the south top perspective maps we will return to C.E. mediaeval expansionary empires because of the extensive reach of trade and travel during that era with the movement of Islam and the late 500s there are already mini African empires stretching completely across the continent of Africa and extensively populated before the Islamic expansion but to our point of documentation it is the story of Islam related to the year of the elephant at its core we continue to reiterate it to validate the psychology of the mind relative to the story that the common African expanding westward pre-Islamic expansion had already been masters of taming training and naming these monstrous beasts. And that should be remembered the compilations in this book of the empires and their interconnectedness, the last great known era to be that of Islam prior to colonialism and the scramble of Africa 1885 Berlin conference. The 9th century to the 19th century in what is now present-day Chad and Nigeria. The empire was home to various ethnic groups, and specific details about all the ethnicities and their languages are limited but here are a few.

Kanembu: The Kanembu people were the dominant ethnic group in the Kanem Empire. Their language, also called Kanembu, belongs to the Nilo-Saharan language family.

Bulala: The Bulala people were a major ethnic group in the Kanem Empire, and they were initially a vassal group under Kanem's rule. They later rebelled and established their dynasty. The language spoken by the Bulala people was likely a Chadic language.

Zaghawa: The Zaghawa people were another significant ethnic group in the region, inhabiting parts of present-day Chad, Sudan, and
Libya. They spoke the Zaghawa language, which belongs to the Saharan branch of the Nilo-Saharan language family.

Bura: The Bura people were primarily concentrated in the Mandara Mountains region, which extends into northern Nigeria. The Bura language is classified as a Biu-Mandara language, belonging to the Afro-Asiatic language family.

Kanuri: While not an indigenous ethnicity of the Kanem Empire, the Kanuri people played a crucial role in the empire's history. They inhabited the neighboring Bornu Empire and eventually conquered Kanem, forming the Kanem-Bornu Empire. The Kanuri language, also known as Kanembu, is a Nilo-Saharan language.

Regarding descriptive words for their regalia, weaponry, armor, metalwork, and literature, it's important to note that detailed information about these aspects may be scarce due to the historical context and limited documentation. However, here are some general descriptors:

Regalia: Elaborate, ceremonial, ornate, colorful, symbolic, beaded, embroidered.

Weaponry: Spears, swords, shields, bows and arrows, daggers, javelins, leather-wrapped handles, decorated pommels.

Armor: Chainmail, lamellar armor, leather armor, metal plates, scales, helmets, shields, decorative motifs. Metalwork: Intricate, filigree, engraved, hammered, embossed, decorative patterns, inlaid with precious materials.

Literature: Oral tradition, epic tales, poetic recitations, folklore, proverbs, songs, riddles, historical accounts, genealogies.

The specific characteristics of regalia, weaponry, armor, metalwork, and literature can vary within and among the different ethnic groups of the Kanem Empire.

The historical connections between the Kanuri language and Arabic are so strong that one may be inclined to accept them. For instance, the way the days of the week are counted in Kanuri is identical to Arabic in terms of both the pattern and names. Thus, the Kanuri weekdays are Litirin, Talau, Larawa, Lamisu, Zuma, Sibdu, and Ladu, while in Arabic, they are Alaithnayn, Althulatha, Al'arbiea, Alkhamis, Aljumat, Alsabt, and Al'ahad (الأحد). There are also similarities in certain words and nouns. For example, "Dunya" in Kanuri is equivalent to "Duniya" in Arabic, both meaning "the World" in their respective languages. Other examples include "Suwanallah" in Kanuri, which corresponds to "Subhannallah" in Arabic, "Sadaa" in Kanuri, which is "Sadaqqa" in Arabic, "Nuwur" in Kanuri, which is "Nur" in Arabic, and "Lardu" in Kanuri, which is "Lard" in Arabic. Similarly, words like "Zannah" (Paradise), "Mairuwu" (Maghrib), "Riman" (Imam), "Sami" (Samai), "Kasuwu" (Suk or Souk), and "Fajar" (Dawn) share commonalities. Additionally, the months of the year in Kanuri are Muaram, Safar,

Rabiyul Awwal, Rabiul Sani, Jummada Awal, Jumada Gaji, Rajab, Shaaban, Ramalam, Shawwal, Zulkidda, and Zulhajj, which are named similarly in Arabic as Muharram, Safar Rabiul Auwwal, Rabius Sani, Jamadial Auwwal, Jamadius Sani, Rajab, Shaban, Ramadan, Shawwal, and Zil Qad Zil Hajj (month of Hajj). Furthermore, historical evidence suggests that the Kanuri people have been using Arabic alphabets and numerals for communication for over a thousand years. Taking all these facts into account, it becomes evident that the Kanuri language is a result of the decayed or decaying local Arabic language mixed with some local African indigenous languages. The name "Kanuri" itself is derived from two Kanuri words: "KA," meaning "Stick," and "NURI," meaning "Light." The word "NURI" is originally derived from the Arabic word "NUR," which also means "Light" in Arabic. Therefore, "KA + NURI = KANURI." The reason behind referring to the Kanuri people as "KA + NURI = KANURI " is that upon their arrival, they were primarily pastoralists engaged in the rearing of cattle and sheep. These animals were herded on foot or with the help of animals such as horses and donkeys.

As is customary among pastoralists, they carried a stick to guide their animals while grazing and bringing them back home. This was also the case for the Kanuri people. However, the Sau people noticed that there were many pastoralists in the area who followed the same pattern of animal husbandry, but the Kanuri people had a noticeably fresher-looking skin. The Kanuri people acquired their name "Kanuri" and became known by various tribes and nations, including the Saus, Arabs, Kotoko, Berbers, Sudanese, Europeans,

Ethiopians, Turks, and Egyptians. They were also recognized by other local ethnic groups, such as the Marghi, Babur, Ngezem, Chibok, Gwoza, and Bolewa. It is worth noting that the Kanuri language was the dominant language of the pre-colonial Kanem-Bornu Empire and continues to be the primary language spoken in Borno and Yobe states in modern-day Nigeria, as well as in Diffa and Damagaram in Niger Republic to this day. This is another illustration of the interconnectedness of the shared movements of people throughout Africa's kingdoms as evidenced in the languages.

(Moorish Phoenician Carthage)

The history of the Moors of Carthage is a saga that intertwines elements of menacing horror and awe-inspiring power. Led by the formidable and dreadful commander Hannibal, their exploits left an indelible mark on the annals of history. In the heart of the ancient city of Carthage, a civilization renowned for its maritime strength and intricate society, the Moors forged a legacy that was both macabre and astonishingly strategic. Hannibal, born in 247 BCE, was the embodiment of sinister brilliance. His father, the renowned Carthaginian general Hamilcar Barca, instilled within him a sense of duty and a desire for vengeance against Rome.

The History of Hannibal, c. 1570 (tapestry)

With an ominous aura surrounding him, Hannibal emerged as a malevolent force to be reckoned with. His name alone evoked a sense of eerie foreboding, and his campaigns were characterised by a haunting mixture of calculated tactics and raw aggression. The Battle of Cannae stands as a chilling testament to Hannibal's

terrifying genius. Employing a double envelopment manoeuvre, he ensnared the Roman legions in a ghastly embrace that led to their monstrous annihilation. This spine-chilling event showcased his intimidating grasp of military strategy and his ability to orchestrate a symphony of gruesome destruction. The very thought of his methods sent shivers down the spines of those who faced him.

The battle of Scipio the African; tapestry woven by Marcus Geeraerts, Quirinal Palace, Rome

41198 - ROMA - Palazzo del Quirinale - Battaglia di Scipione - M. Geerarts - Arazzo - (Stab. Soc. D. Anderson - Roma).

Hannibal's audacious invasion of Rome, accomplished by crossing the Alps with war elephants, was a feat that exuded both fearsome power and strategic brilliance. His forces, accompanied by these enormous beasts, carried an air of dominating strength as they marched through treacherous terrain. The war elephants, equipped with their towering regalia, were a spectacle of overpowering force that added to the commanding presence of Hannibal's army.

The war elephants, with their armored hide and towering towers, were both formidable and majestic, a combination that struck terror into the hearts of his enemies. Their overwhelming size and potent presence on the battlefield were a testament to Hannibal's tyrannical ability to manipulate both man and beast to his advantage. The very sight of these savage creatures became a symbol of his unyielding resolve to conquer.

Amidst the blood and chaos, the Phoenician language, spoken by the Carthaginians, carried echoes of an ancient heritage. The ancestral roots of this language tied it to the city's rich history, and its influence was far-reaching. Interestingly, the Phoenician language held a connection to the origin of the English alphabet. The Phoenicians, credited with the development of one of the earliest known alphabets, laid the groundwork for writing systems that would evolve into the very alphabet used in the English language today. The Phoenician language's mysterious symbols, initially representing consonant sounds, evolved into the more complex writing systems of Greek and Latin. These changes, in turn, influenced the development of the English alphabet. This

linguistic evolution, though subtle, carried profound implications. It was a journey that transformed the Phoenician symbols into the intellectual foundation of modern communication.

Counts:
Hannibal's forces consisted of approximately 50,000 infantry and 10,000 cavalry. He also deployed around 80 war elephants in his formation. The infantry included a mix of Carthaginians, Numidians, and other allied troops.

The Roman army, commanded by Consuls Lucius Aemilius Paullus and Gaius Terentius Varro, numbered around 86,000 infantry and 6,000 cavalry. The Roman infantry comprised Roman citizens and allied troops from various parts of the Republic.

Battle Duration:
The Battle of Cannae unfolded for a single day. It is said that the battle began early in the morning and lasted until late in the afternoon.

Losses and Outcome:
The battle resulted in a stunning and devastating victory for Hannibal's forces. Despite being vastly outnumbered, Hannibal's strategic brilliance allowed him to encircle and annihilate the Roman legions. The Romans suffered an estimated 50,000 to 70,000 casualties, with some sources suggesting even higher numbers. This included not only fatalities but also captured soldiers.

The magnificent Flemish Tapestry in Palazzo del Quirinale in Rome
that portrays a meeting between Scipio the Elder Africanus
(236–183 BC) and Hannibal (247– c. 183/181 BC).

Hannibal's losses were comparatively much lighter, with estimates
varying between 5,000 and 8,000 casualties. Amid the horror and
power that defined Hannibal's era, the role of intelligence was
ever-present. Hannibal himself was not just a wielder of potent

force; he was also a master tactician, displaying astute decision-making and analytical prowess. His ingenious maneuvers were calculated to exploit the weaknesses of his adversaries, and his discerning mind meticulously dissected the battlefield.

Hannibal's legacy was that of a commander who seamlessly blended cunning strategy with raw intellect. His resourceful approaches to challenges demonstrated a kind of brilliance that went beyond conventional tactics. His perceptive understanding of his enemies allowed him to stay several steps ahead, like a sharp predator stalking its prey. His campaigns were not just displays of force; they were symphonies of wisdom in motion.

The tale of the Moors of Carthage, under Hannibal's guidance, stands as a complex tapestry woven with threads of horrifying conquests, commanding power, and intellectual mastery. It's a story that continues to captivate, offering lessons on the intricate interplay of vile force and brilliant strategy. The echoes of their endeavors remind us that history is often a convergence of the terrifying and the intelligent, a blend of the sinister and the astute.

The Battle of Cannae, one of the most infamous clashes in ancient history, occurred during the Second Punic War between the Carthaginian forces led by Hannibal and the Roman Republic. The battle took place on August 2, 216 BCE.

The Battle of Zama (Africa, Second Punic War, 202 BC) won by
Scipio the African over the troops of Hannibal Barca.

Prisoners and Slaves:

The number of Roman soldiers captured during the battle was
substantial. Most estimates place the number of Roman prisoners
taken by the Carthaginians at around 20,000 to 30,000. These
prisoners were subsequently sold into slavery, contributing to the
workforce of Carthage and other territories.

The Battle of Cannae is often cited as one of the most strategically
brilliant victories in military history due to Hannibal's innovative
tactics. His ability to use a double envelopment maneuver to
encircle and crush a much larger Roman force demonstrated his
mastery of the battlefield and strategic thinking. The battle had a

profound impact on the course of the Second Punic War, altering the balance of power between Carthage and Rome.

At a second glance when you look at the numbers, you would see that it is reported to have lost 70,000 men and factoring in the reported enslavement 20 or 30,000 men sold into slavery on the continent of Africa. One can see that the majority of the Romans literally gave up. But still, it is counted as the battle of annihilation counting even those who have been enslaved to be dead and lost to Africa. These are hard histories and worth it to be remembered. and studied to understand human nature, politics and war.

The transformation of the ancient Phoenician alphabet into the modern English alphabet is a remarkable journey that spans centuries and civilizations. The origins of the alphabet can be traced back to the Semitic Phoenicians, who inhabited the coastal regions of the eastern Mediterranean, including modern-day Lebanon. The Phoenicians are credited with developing one of the earliest known alphabets, a significant departure from the earlier hieroglyphic and logographic writing systems.

At its inception, the Phoenician alphabet consisted of a relatively small set of symbols, each representing a consonant sound. Unlike the intricate hieroglyphic languages that utilized intricate pictures to convey meanings, the Phoenician script was concise and efficient. Each symbol represented a single sound, allowing for a more streamlined and practical approach to written communication.

This simplicity and versatility were key factors that contributed to the spread of the Phoenician alphabet to other cultures and languages. As the Phoenician traders and sailors navigated the Mediterranean, their script was adopted by various peoples, each modifying it to suit their own linguistic needs. This gave rise to the development of different scripts and writing systems, such as the Greek and Latin alphabets, both of which have had a profound influence on the modern English alphabet.

The Greek adaptation of the Phoenician alphabet marked a significant milestone in its evolution. The Greeks introduced vowel sounds, which were absent in the original Phoenician script. This addition expanded the expressive potential of the alphabet, enabling it to more accurately represent the intricacies of spoken language. The Greek alphabet eventually became the foundation for numerous languages, including Latin.

The Roman Empire's rise brought the Latin alphabet to the forefront of cultural and linguistic development. This script, which had evolved from the Phoenician symbols, became the basis for many languages across Europe. The Latin alphabet, in turn, evolved into various forms, each adapting to the unique phonetic nuances of the language it represented.

The English language, in its journey from Old English to Middle English and finally to Modern English, experienced significant linguistic shifts that were mirrored in the evolution of its alphabet. The English alphabet comprises 26 letters, each representing both

consonant and vowel sounds. This rich set of symbols is a testament to the adaptability and enduring nature of the ancient Phoenician script.

While the modern English alphabet has undergone numerous changes, its core owes a debt of gratitude to the Phoenician script and its subsequent adaptations. The essence of concise representation, where each letter corresponds to a specific sound, remains a fundamental principle of the English writing system. This transformation from the elaborate hieroglyphic language of symbols to the pragmatic and adaptable English alphabet highlights the dynamic nature of language evolution and the enduring influence of the Phoenician legacy.

The journey from the Semitic Phoenician script to the modern English alphabet is astounding. The shift from complex hieroglyphs to a concise phonetic script marked a pivotal moment in human history, enabling the exchange of ideas and information on a scale previously unattainable. The adaptability of the Phoenician alphabet allowed it to be embraced by various cultures and languages, ultimately laying the foundation for the diverse array of scripts in use today.

To argue history in the English language concerning its meaning and etymology proves to be entirely futile. The arrangement of its structure has emerged over time due to contemporary conquests, rather than being grounded in the phonetics of its etymological roots.

When delving into the extensive field of linguistics and narratives encompassing the origins of the English language, particularly its Germanic and French influences, it becomes evident that the English language, concerning its letters and phonetic sounds, lacks unequivocal significance. Instead, it stands as a collection of letters and sounds devoid of inherent definition. These components possess no intrinsic meaning; they merely contribute to generating sounds. This absence of inherent meaning is precisely why engaging in historical debates within the context of the English language becomes an exercise in absurdity.

It is widely acknowledged that the manipulation of letters and sounds in the English language lacks any inherent depth. This manipulation often seeks to imitate elements from ancient civilizations and languages, devoid of the substantial meaning that can be attributed to those sources. Excellent portrayal and commerce and technology as it is widespread and understood. Although through the means of conquests and imposition of religion. When discussing history, it is best to use the language of the people which is the topic of discussion. It is said that there are so many instances with events and ideas do not translate if the language is not the language of the land. The profound interconnectedness of the Berber tribes, particularly the astute Numidian tribes of African birth and indigenous African heritage, played an instrumental role in the conquest of Rome. These tribes, renowned for their intellectual prowess and strategic genius, were key participants in a historical narrative that reshaped the course of civilizations.

The Numidian tribes, deeply rooted in their African origins, forged a bond of unity as they embarked on the strategic conquest of Rome. Their names resonated across history, carrying the weight of their shared ancestry and the lands they held dear. Through their collective efforts, they achieved a victory that would serve as a testament to their intellectual brilliance for generations to come. As Carthage's influence extended beyond the Mediterranean, its legacy reached even the distant coasts of the Atlantic. The significance of this era is underscored by the intriguing discovery of Phoenician writings in far-flung regions, including the Americas. These inscriptions stand as a testament to the intellectual and strategic reach of Carthage, tracing the paths of its explorers and traders.

The conquest of Carthage, with the participation of the Berber and Numidian tribes, marked a pivotal moment in the histories of both Africa and Rome. The return of plundered wealth to the African continent added a layer of complexity to the intercontinental interactions of the time. It reflected the strategic prowess of these tribes and their commitment to shaping their destinies. The Berber and Numidian tribes not only played an active role in shaping history but also illuminated the intricate nature of cultural exchange. Their stories highlight that the narratives of nations are often woven together, influenced by cooperation and negotiation. The legacy of their involvement in the Carthaginian conquest and its aftermath resonates as a testament to the intellectual brilliance and strategic genius that transcends borders, leaving an enduring mark on the pages of time.

Chapter 5
Origin of Moorish Islam In Africa

Exert
Evliya Çelebi
-Gifts from the Berberi King to The Sultan

" I spent three days here conversing with the king. Then the governor took the booty of Kör Husayn Qan, the King of Hafir, and the Berberi king prepared the gifts that he was sending to the Sultan of Funjistan as well as the 1,000 camels, 70 elephants, 1,000 cattle, 6,000 sheep, and 500 fireworshipping and Magian captives"

We **now return to Ethiopia** and we double back for the sole reason addressing the Islamic expansion and the origins protections that Ethiopia gave the Islamic prophet Muhammad. In this, we will address two matters, that of the raining and ruling Axumite families of Abyssinia at that time and we will address The progenitor of the Mali empire, Bilal Al Habesha in the next segment. And to start we will start with this.

Axumite kings, starting with Caleb and ending with the Negus who provided refuge to Muhammad: As of the last mentioned Axumite king in the list, Menelik II, the historical context changed, and the Axumite kingdom transitioned into the Ethiopian Empire. The king

who provided refuge to Muhammad is not explicitly mentioned in the list as the Negus who provided refuge to Muhammad was Ashama ibn Abjar, also known as An-Najashi. This event took place before the reigns of the kings mentioned in the list.

During the time of Muhammad, the king of Ethiopia was Ashama ibn Abjar, also known as An-Najashi. This story is often referred to as the "Migration to Abyssinia" or the "First Hijra."
Muhammad and his followers faced persecution and opposition in Mecca from the Quraysh tribe, who opposed his teachings. In the year 615 AD, Muhammad advised a group of his followers to seek refuge in the Kingdom of Aksum (Ethiopia) under the rule of King Ashama. The group, which included both Muslims and their families, fled to Ethiopia to escape the oppression they were facing.

Upon their arrival, the Quraish sent a delegation to King Ashama, seeking the return of the Muslims. King Ashama summoned the Muslim refugees to his court to understand their situation. In response, the Muslim' spokesperson, Ja'far ibn Abi Talib, explained their reasons for seeking refuge in Ethiopia and recited the letter that Prophet Muhammad had sent to King Ashama. The letter reads as follows:

"In the name of Allah, the Most Gracious, the Most Merciful. From Muhammad, the Messenger of Allah, to Al-Najashi, king of Abyssinia. Peace be upon you, O king! I praise Allah, the One, and Only God, the Eternal, the Absolute. He begets not, nor is He begotten. There is none like unto Him. I bear witness that Jesus, the

son of Mary, is the spirit of God and His Word which He cast into Mary, the virgin, the good, the pure, so that she conceived Jesus. Allah created him from His spirit and His breathing as He created Adam by His hand. I call you to Allah, the Unique, without a partner, and to His obedience and to follow me and to believe in that which came to me, for I am the Messenger of Allah. I invite you and your men to Allah, the Glorious, the All-Mighty. I hereby bear witness that I have communicated my message and advice. I invite you to listen and accept my advice. Peace be upon him who follows true guidance."

King Ashama was moved by the words of the letter and the testimony of Ja'far. He refused to hand over the Muslims to the Quraysh and assured their safety under his protection. He provided them sanctuary and treated them with respect during their stay in Ethiopia.

The story of King Ashama's compassionate response to Muhammad's followers seeking refuge in his kingdom is seen as an example of religious tolerance and compassion. This event is also significant in Islamic history as one of the early instances of Muslims seeking protection in a non-Muslim land, highlighting the importance of safety and justice irrespective of religious beliefs. These are the origins of Islam on the continent of Africa.

The spread of Islam in various directions, and the Moorish Empire closely resembled this pattern.

1. Arab Tribes' Expansion into Africa:
The Arab tribes' expansion into Africa was a gradual process driven by trade, migration, and conquest. These tribes established trade networks that penetrated the African continent, especially along the eastern coast and into the Nile Valley. Key Arab tribes involved in this expansion include the Quraish, Banu Hashim, and Banu Umayya.
Their influence laid the foundation for cultural, religious, and economic interactions between Arab and African communities.

2. Spread of Islam in Various Directions:
After the emergence of Islam in the 7th century, its teachings spread rapidly, leading to the expansion of Islamic territories in different directions:

Southwards: The Swahili coast of East Africa and the Comoros islands became centers of Islamic trade and culture.
Westwards: North Africa, including modern-day Morocco, Tunisia, Algeria, and Libya, converted to Islam.

3. The Moorish Empire and Invasion of Spain:
The Moors, a term used to describe Muslim inhabitants of North Africa and Iberia, played a significant role in the history of the Moorish Empire. The Umayyad Caliphate's fall led to the establishment of various emirates and dynasties in North Africa, particularly the Fatimids and the Almoravids.

Al-Andalus: The Umayyad Caliphate's remnants established a flourishing Muslim state in Spain known as Al-Andalus. The Moors introduced advanced irrigation techniques, architecture, mathematics, and philosophy to the Iberian Peninsula.

- **Tariq ibn Ziyad**: The Islamic conquest of Spain by the Umayyad general Tariq ibn Ziyad in 711 AD marked a significant event. The Battle of Guadalete and the subsequent expansion of

Venetian School, 18th century Allegories of the four continents-
Africa.
Description

Moorish group of Africans together in traditional Moorish North African red headdress and feather to African Moors mounted on African elephant

Muslim rule paved the way for the establishment of the Umayyad Emirate in Al-Andalus.
4. Influence of the Moors and War Elephants:
The Moors' influence in Al-Andalus extended across various fields:

- **Technology and Science**: The Moors introduced advanced technologies and scientific knowledge to Al-Andalus, which influenced fields such as astronomy, medicine, and architecture. Their contributions laid the groundwork for the European Renaissance.

- **Cultural Exchange**: The Moors facilitated cultural exchange between the Islamic world, Europe, and Africa. The city of Cordoba became a hub of learning and diversity.

War Elephants: While war elephants were not a central feature of the Moorish military, they had historical significance. Some earlier North African dynasties, like the Carthaginians, had used war elephants in their military campaigns. However, the Moors' military success was not primarily reliant on these animals.

5. Tribes' Participation in North African Affairs: Various tribes and dynasties played roles in North African history:

Berbers: Indigenous Berber tribes inhabited North Africa before and during Islamic expansion. They interacted with Arab conquerors and sometimes resisted or allied with them.

Almoravids: The Almoravid dynasty emerged among the Sanhaja Berber tribes in the Sahara and played a vital role in unifying and defending North African territories.

Almohads: The Almohad dynasty succeeded the Almoravids and expanded their influence across North Africa and Al-Andalus.

Merinids: The Merinid dynasty originated from the Zenata Berber tribe and ruled Morocco and parts of North Africa.

Berber Tribes, Jewish Communities, and Queen Kahina that resisted engaging in many battles with the Islamic expansions are:
Berbers: The Berber tribes, indigenous to North Africa, engaged in various resistances against different empires, including the
Romans, Vandals, Byzantines, and Islamic forces. They often defended their lands, cultures, and identities against foreign rulers.

Jewish Communities: Jewish communities across North Africa also resisted Islamic expansion and other empires. Notable communities were present in places like Morocco, Tunisia, and Algeria. They faced various challenges, including religious and cultural differences.

Queen Kahina (Dihya): An iconic figure in Berber history, Queen Kahina was a Berber Jewish leader who played a pivotal role in resisting the Islamic Umayyad conquests in the 7th century. Her leadership and military strategies made her a symbol of Berber resistance.

Use of War Elephants and Battles:
Battles of Resistance with War Elephants:
Battle of Tangier (708 AD): Berber resistance against the Umayyad Caliphate. Although war elephants were not prominently documented in this battle, they were sometimes used by Berber forces.

Battle of the Nobles (740 AD): Berbers resisted the Umayyad Caliphate's rule in North Africa. While the use of war elephants is not well-documented in this battle, their sporadic presence in Berber armies could be assumed.

Battle of Bagdoura (744 AD): Berbers resisted Umayyad forces. The employment of war elephants is uncertain, but they could
have been utilized to varying degrees.

Africa
" Africa from a set of The Four Continents - tapestry by Jean Jacques François Le Barbier" (1738-1826)

Battle of Rasil (644 AD): Berber tribes resisted against the Rashidun Caliphate's expansion. War elephants were sporadically used by Berber forces in various engagements.

Battle of Sufetula (647 AD): Berbers resisted the Rashidun Caliphate. War elephants were employed by both sides and their use impacted the course of the battle.

Battle of Xerigordon (1989): Berber rebels resisted the Fatimid Caliphate. While war elephants were not a central feature of this conflict, their presence in North African battles is evident.

Queen Kahina's Campaigns: Queen Kahina's leadership included military strategies against Islamic expansion. While specific battles with war elephants aren't recorded, her efforts underscore the diversity of Berber resistance tactics.

The historical records from this period can be fragmentary, and the extent of war elephants' participation in specific battles might vary. Queen Kahina's role as a Berber Jewish leader and her campaigns

against the Umayyads demonstrate the complexity of resistance efforts in North Africa.

I can provide you with a general list of some of the rulers of the Kingdom of Makuria and their approximate reign periods. However, please note that historical records from this period can be fragmentary and incomplete, so specific details might vary.

King Merkurios (c. 8th century): One of the earliest rulers of the Christian kingdom of Makuria. Little is known about his reign.

King Zacharias (c. 8th century): Also known as Za Zacharias, he ruled during a period of Nubian-Christian-Islamic interactions.

King Kyriakos (9th century): Reigned during a time of increased contact and conflict with Islamic powers to the north.

King Abraham (10th century): His reign saw continued efforts to defend against Islamic expansion into Nubian territory.

King George (10th century): Ruled during a time of political and military challenges, with Islamic forces attempting to exert
influence.

King David (c. 10th–11th century): His reign marked a period of further challenges from Islamic forces, including invasions and conflicts.

King Samuel (11th century): Samuel's reign was marked by continued interactions with Islamic powers and efforts to defend Nubian territory.

King Ezekiel (11th century): His reign saw Nubia dealing with both Islamic pressures and internal challenges.

In many cases, I am surprised to find as much information as I have found during research of these eras. In the studies of history, it is easily observable to see how the dominating empire diminishes the value and worth of the empire and defeat. Any positive records or destroyed all negative records or magnified to create the narratives, negativity and the illusion or justification of an invasion force. However, it should be noted that it is said that the majority of the expansion of Islam in Africa was not due to Asian influence but that of the Africans with Asian assistance.

But closely embracing our illustrious journey through the Islamic expansion into the African continent, led by native Africans, sets the stage for extensive discussions about the Moorish empires and kingdoms intertwined with Saharan ancestries. This exploration will be further unfolded in the upcoming second edition. These

historical narratives and empires possess a complex and interconnected nature, existing alongside the real-time events of their era that significantly shaped world history.

The Moorish empires spanning Spain, Morocco, and Northern West Africa emerge as central players in Western history, their roles reverberating across time. The forthcoming edition will briefly touch on their impact on the Atlantic migrational expansion. This topic, deserving a more thorough exploration, will be revisited in the second edition. The intricacies of these events demand on-the-ground research and direct translations to capture the accurate essence of people's lives and ancestries, enriched by a multitude of oral traditions and narratives. Now on to Ghana!

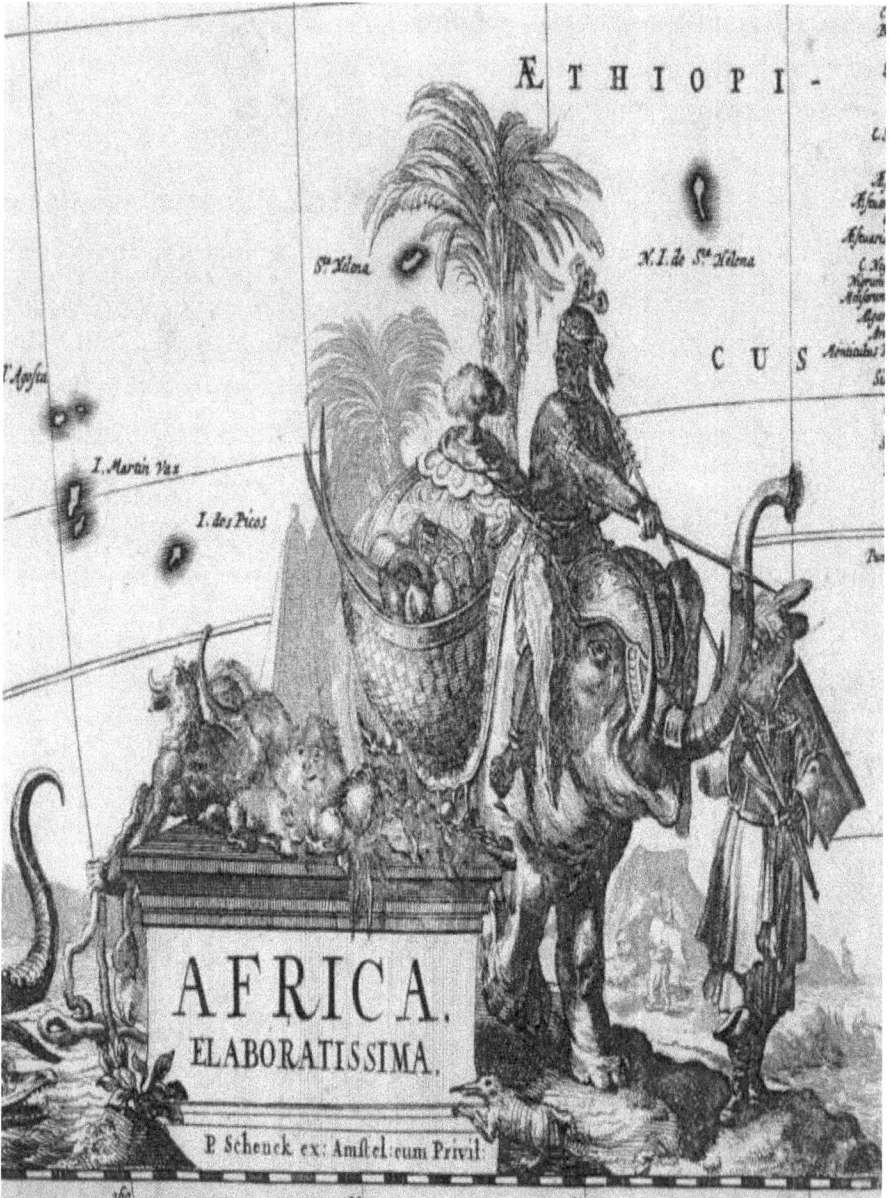

This map of Africa, issued by Pieter Schenk in his Atlas Contractus, shows many of the common cartographic myths about the continent prevalent through the 19th century. Two St. Helena islands can be found in the Atlantic Ocean. The Niger River is pictured as an extension of Senegal, connected to the dumbbell pattern of Lacus Guarde and Borno Lacus (the latter being a close geographic approximation to Lake Tchad). Additional large bodies of water are seen in the southern portion of the continent, corresponding to the Ptolemaic tradition of the source of the Nile.

The most accurate information can be found on the coasts, with the names of various ports and navigable rivers tightly grouped densely in the northwest; along the Ivory, Gold, and Grain Coasts. A decorative cartouche immediately catches the eye in the lower left, prominently showing an armored elephant, obelisks, and heavily adorned natives. Schenk, along with his brother-in-law Gerard Valk, purchased the plates of other Dutch mapmakers like Johannes Janssonius to expedite the creation of their composite atlases. This appears to be an original work, though the interior detail is heavily influenced by predecessors. 1705

Chapter 6
Ghana Mali Niger

Akan proverb
"When an elephant steps on a trap it fails to spring back"

"**Mansa Musa observed one** of the five pillars of Islam by undertaking a pilgrimage to Mecca (known as Hajj). When he embarked on his Hajj in 1324, he travelled thousands of miles across treacherous terrain with 60,000 people, 21,000 kilograms of gold, 100 elephants and 80 camels"

" The Desert Elephant"

"While you might hear it said on geographical channels, specials, or even in textbooks that there are two African elephants—the bush elephant (*Loxodonta africana*) and the forest elephant (*Loxodonta cyclotis*)—in actuality, there are three distinct African elephants. The desert elephant (*Loxodonta africana africana*) is a subspecies found in Namibia, Ghana, Mali, and even parts of Sudan and Chad. This subspecies has evolved unique adaptations to survive in challenging desert conditions, setting it apart from its counterparts. Their adaptations include elongated legs to cover more ground with each step, a larger and more concave skull to regulate body temperature, and a modified body shape for more efficient thermoregulation in extreme heat.

BESCHRYVINGE
Van de
Goudt - Kust
GUINEA.
Als mede een Voyagie naer de selve.

Waer in den Aert des Landts / Koopmanschap / Handeling / Gedierten /
Vogelen / Visschen / Boomen / Kruyden / Bergwerck / Mineralia of Goudt-
soecking / Nature, Gestaldt / Kleedinge / Geloove / Steeden / Huysen /
Leven / Gewoonten / en Visscherye der Swarten en Inwoon-
ders des selven Landts / seer duydelijck beschreven
worden / Door P. D. M.

't AMSTERDAM,
By Joost Hartgers, Boeck-verkoper op den Dam / bezijden het Stadthuys /
op de hoeck van de Kalver-straet / in de Boeck-winckel. 1650.

INTRODUCING "DESCRIPTIONS AND HISTORICAL ACCOUNT
OF THE GOLDEN KINGDOM OF GUINEA" BY PIETER DE
MAREES: An early 17th century publication on the Gold Coast
J. B. Ammissah and J. B. Amissah

202

Despite being a subcategory of the bush elephant, which is the largest of them all, the desert elephant has developed specific traits to thrive in arid environments. These adaptations have allowed them to locate and dig for water in dry riverbeds and access vegetation that other elephants might not be able to reach.

Jacopo Amigoni 1765 Description

Two Africans on a shore, one on the left kneeling with one foot in the water and plants in his hand, the other standing, holding a spear and looking up at a third man who passes, riding a laden elephant; a palm tree, lion and elephant in the background;

- Inscription type: inscription
- Inscription content: Lettered below the image with the title, in four lines of verse, and 'Amiconi Pinx,,t // Moor Fecit. // London Printed for & Sold by R. Sayer opposite Fetter lane Fleet Street.' Verses: 'Gold, Iv'ry, Coral, Africa may boast, / But whilst those regions feel too fierce a blaze / And brute-like Natives blacken all the Coast, / They more our Pity, than our Envy, raise.'

Notice the sheer detail in the illustration and depiction of the Moorish guard and the laborer as well as the mounted elephant and laborer carrying goods and adorned in cloths and elements of armor In times past, when empires reigned, these desert elephants held immense value. They are believed to be the very elephants Mansa Musa, the ruler of the Mali Empire, used during his historic desert journey to Mecca. Beyond the Mali Empire, these elephants played roles in the desert civilizations of Sudan and Chad, as well as the Moorish empires. Unfortunately, much of their population has diminished due to modernization and human development. This could explain the limited mention of these remarkable creatures in historical accounts."

Ghana will be the western most prominent topic of discussion, it is the ancient Ghana of old that predates modern Ghana but the nations of people that make up Ghana in their respective empires and states and lineages and kingdoms and migrations are indeed foundations of the old Ghana. And with Ghana as the westernmost Royal African ancestrial family we tie into the empires of Mali and Shanghai and the predating of Ghana to the Phoenician Carthage Empire of ancient North West Africa and the most feared general in human history. Second to Nimrod the son of Kush would be Hannibal Barker of Cottage who himself launched the most studied invasion in history and the most decisive battle. Military tacticians have deemed the battle of annihilation. But we begin this chapter in the west of the Kanem Banu Empire and address Ghana.

It is said that The Empire of Ghana formed in 300 AD when different tribes of the Soninke people were united under the first king, Dinga Cisse. The Soninke people used the word 'Ghana', meaning 'Warrior King' to refer to the king, and the Empire's enemies and allies subsequently began to refer to the region as 'Ghana'. The word, Ghana means warrior or war chief and was the title given to the rulers of the original kingdom whose Soninke name was Ouagadou. Kaya Maghan (King of Gold) was another title for these kings. From this juncture, we will create a perspective based on the folklore historical heritage and customs of the people of Ghana.

Exert
al-Hasan Ibn Muhammad Ibn Ahmad al-Wazzan (Descriptions of Africa)

"The five peoples of Libya divided these countries into fifteen divisions, so each people obtained three of them. The fact is that the current King of Techno, Abu Bakr Askia of the black race, had been appointed commander-in-chief by the King of Timbuktu and Kago Suni Ali, who is of Libyan origin (2).

After the death of Sunni Ali, Abu Bakr revolted against his sons and killed them, and then he saved all the black people from the yoke of the chiefs of the tribes of Libya, so that he seized several kingdoms in a matter of six years, and when he finished spreading peace and tranquillity in his kingdom Sunni (2) There are two rulers from the Mina family, each of whom is called Mina Ali - and the Sudanese write it with Ya: Mina, and without it Mina - the first of which is known as Mina Klan. The external oppressor, the immoral, and the last of the Meni family who was

fired after his death, Muhammad Askia, the founder of the Eskirian state, the rulers of the region until the advent of the armies of Ahmad al-Mansur, and the family's state continued from the year

735-1335 to the year 1493/898, successively ruling during these four years, the rulers of the region 71 See: Abd Al-Rahman Al-Saadi, History of Sudan, p

160 Ibn Hawqal, writing in 951 on trade and the importance of salt.

Awdaghust is a former Berber town in current Mauritania. It was an important oasis in the Southern end of the caravan route.

"The King of Awdaghust maintains relations with the King of Ghana.[The King of] Ghana is the wealthiest king on the face of the earth because of his treasures and stocks of gold extracted in olden times for his predecessors and himself. [...] They stand in oppressing the need of [the goodwill of] the kings of Awdaghust because of the salt which comes to them from the lands of Islam. They cannot do without this salt, of which one land, in the interior and more remote parts of the land of Sudan, may fetch between 200 and 300 Dinars"

AFRICA.

C. le Brun pinxit.   *le Blond excudit.*   *Earl Beullett sculebit.*

Africa

Title: 4 Hand-colored Engraved Allegorical Plates ...

The king of Ghana, when he calls up his army, can put 200,000 men into the field, more than 40,000 of them archers."
The comprehensive library Book of Tracts and Kingdoms of Bakri [Abu Ubaid al-Bakri]

Volume Two [The Road from Ghana to Tadamkeh] [The road from Ghana to Tadmakah]

Africa, published c.1790" by G. Wagner

"1472 As for the avenue from Ghana to Tadamkeh, and there is a distance of fifty (1) days between them, from Ghana to Sfengo there are three stages, and it is on the Nile, and it is the last work of Ghana. (To Tadamakra, and between them is a twenty-day journey). Then you

accompany the Nile to Bograt, in which there is a tribe from Sanhaja known as Madasa. The jurist (Abu Muhammad) «3» told Abd al-Malik that he saw in Bograt a bird that looked like a hook, and every listener could understand from its voice an unambiguous understanding: The killing of Hussein, the killing of Hussein, he repeats over and over, then says:

Karbala once. Abd al-Malik said: I and the Muslims who attended with me heard it.

And from Bograt to Tirqi. Then you walk from it in the desert to Tadamkeh, and Tadamkeh is more like the country of the world to Makkah (God honored it and increased it in honor and glorification) «4». (And the meaning of Tad for them is a form since it is in the form of Mecca) «5», and it is a large city between mountains and reefs, and it is better built than the city of Ghana and the city of Coco.

The people of Tadamkeh are Berber Muslims, and they excavate as (6) the Berbers of the desert, and their livelihood is from meat and milk and grain that the earth grows without relying on, and corn and all other grains are brought to them from the countries of Sudan, and they wear dyed clothes (with redness from cotton) (7) and Nauli and other than that, And their king wears a red turban, a yellow shirt, and blue pants. And their dinars are called bald because they are pure gold, not sealed.

And their women are exceedingly beautiful, they are not equal to the people of a good country, and for them adultery is permissible, and they hasten to the merchants which of them to carry to her home." Again, to the point of the interconnectedness of African peoples and kingdoms and migrations, we find the melting pot of cultures and identities present in not only Ghana but in the nations of the continent of Africa. Ghana is a residence of Ewe, Akan, Asante people, Volta, Fante, Hausa, Mande, Gurma, Hausa people, Guang, Mossi people, Gonja, Dagbani, Mamprusi,

Dyula, Akyem, Tem, Dangme, though being the home specifically to some and others having modern migration and others pre-colonial migrations it is one of the most diverse and open nations in the continent. Reopening its arms to the diasporic peoples descendant to those of the Holocaust experienced by black people specifically at the beginning of the Spanish Inquisition and the expulsions of Moorish Jewish populations of Spain beginning in 1492 resulting in a Western hemispheric surge for servitude to be inflicted on African peoples.

In this region of ancient Ghana, we find the foundations of the Future rising. Empires and between them the sway of powers over the Northern trade routes through the Sahara to the north and the balances of power and the most peculiar ways and territorial relationships of migrating people.

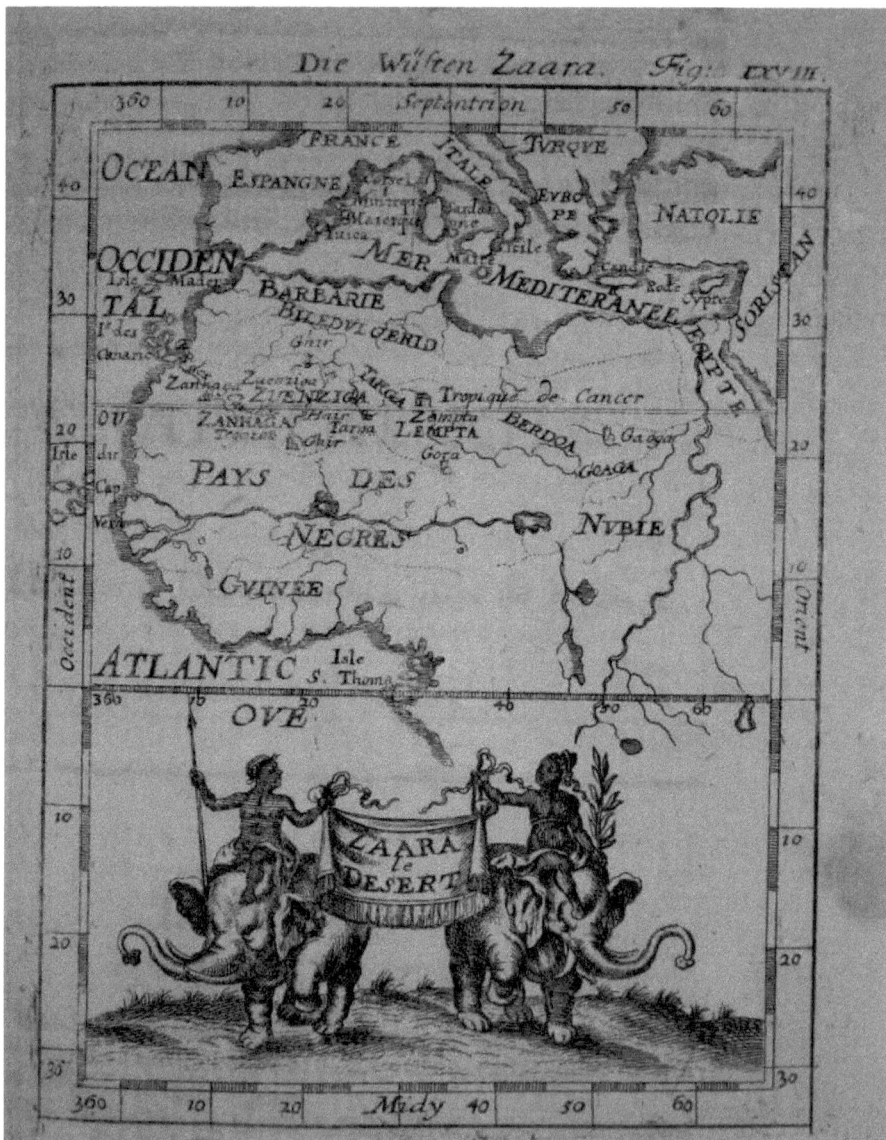

Zaara le desert

Mallet Allain Manesson (1630-1706) Published by Deserto del Sahara, 1719 Representing the Niger and Saharan people

According to tradition, mentioned in the book (Between Rhetoric and Reality The State and Use of Indigenous Knowly Dee)
Edited by Munyaradzi Mawere & Samuel Awuah-Nyamekyethe first chief of Eguafo, Nana Kwamina Ansa I, rode an elephant. As this tradition was stated being a chief and head of state connects royalty to the elephant procession and ceremonial use of the elephant and we will see furthermore the use of elephant resources as adornments and symbols of wealth and medicinal purposes. An Old Ningo tradition asserts that an elephant carried one of their ancestors to safety when he was abandoned after a war. Although details of customs and traditions can vary, it's important to understand the context of what you hear and what you don't hear is also related.

Some elements of legends as we stated before are altered for different reasons or other parts are left out for different reasons but still, the base of the understanding is transmitted in the lessons or the tails of wisdom. It states…." that The man fell asleep on the back of the elephant and the animal took him to a river."But in the future and it's and my travels to document African histories and to be chronologicalized in world history is the essence of this work. Osudoku tradition also holds that elephants were used and cleared the way for the ancestors during their migration to settle at their present abode.

The African Royal Elephant is the true King of the jungle. Throughout time and millennia, the elephant has been a royal symbol of African royalty and of war and wisdom. To African people, the elephant has been a prominent part of The makeup of the civilization of the continent seeing that all creation stories agree, that man was created last and everything else of earth and beast was before so it is the man that enters the territory to live with the elephant and the elephant is not afraid as it knows the land is his and mankind has come to live with him.

In the vast Western territories of the Ghana Empire and the interconnectedness with the regions or what would soon be Mali and that have been in and that of Songhai and into the parts of Nigeria, where there are also artifacts of a Nigerian Warrior King Oba Akenzua I, and artifacts depicting his victory military campaigns against his enemies. Oba Akenzua stands triumphantly on an elephant holding a miniature ukhurhe and a stone axe head, an object associated with warfare. Leopards are also a symbol of royalty in Benin art, and the elephant on either side suggests the Oba's power. As one of the prominent Nigerian kingdoms known for its association with elephants in folklore stories, the Benin Kingdom, in present-day Edo State, Nigeria, has a rich history and

mythology that often includes references to kings or warriors utilizing elephants in battle.

When hearing the traditional accounts and recounts of the histories According to folklore, of Oba (King) of Benin, who was considered a divine ruler, and possessed a special ability to tame elephants it should be clearly understood that as a ruler and warrior king, that certain structural organization is implied, as in reality, things just don't happen by accident. The tradition says that Oba could communicate with and control elephants, and they played a significant role in the kingdom's military campaigns. These stories often depict the elephants as powerful allies in warfare, capable of trampling enemies and causing havoc on the battlefield.

Furthermore, understanding the stories of folklore and tradition there is a certain level that one has comprehended that goes without saying. Understanding kingdoms are made up of classes of peoples, guilds and specialties workers and professionals, clans, tribes, and skills as we mentioned previously. Specifically in Western African kingdoms where members of particular families, through whom the skill is handed down, and they live and work, make up the Benin Kingdom. Other early guilds included physicians, diviners, ironsmiths, carvers, carpenters, and clothmakers. Hunters were also considered professionals and the leopard and elephant hunters had their guilds such as was common in civilization from kingdom to kingdom.

Taking possession of Lake Chad (Africa), 1897: the French steamer " Leon Blot" from the Gentil expedition arrives in Lake Chad to the great amazement of the indigenous people. Illustration in " le Pelerin" of June 12, 1898. by Unknown Artist, (19th century); Private Collection; (add.info.: Taking possession of Lake Chad (Africa), 1897: the French steamer " Leon Blot" from the Gentil expedition arrives in Lake Chad to

the great amazement of the indigenous people. Illustration in " le Pelerin" of June 12, 1898.); Stefano Bianchetti;
King Oba battle folklore

In the ancient land of Benin, there existed a powerful and wise king named Oba. His kingdom was renowned for its wealth, artistry, and military prowess. Across the vast expanse of the land, other kings and kingdoms sought to challenge Oba's supremacy.

One such rival was King Adeolu of the neighboring kingdom of Ijebu. King Adeolu was known for his ambitious nature and his desire to expand his realm. He cast his envious gaze upon the prosperous lands of Benin and sought to conquer them

News of King Adeolu's intentions reached the wise ears of King Oba. Determined to protect his kingdom and people, Oba rallied his warriors and devised a brilliant battle strategy. It was said that Oba had a deep connection with the animal kingdom, and his most loyal companions were the majestic elephants.

Oba summoned his trusted elephant handlers, who had an extraordinary bond with these gentle giants. Together, they embarked on a mission to gather a formidable force of elephants, ensuring their presence on the battlefield.

As King Adeolu's army approached the borders of Benin, they were met with a sight they had never witnessed before. King Oba, astride his mighty war elephant, led his warriors into battle. The ground shook beneath the weight of the charging elephants, their tusks glinting in the sun as they advanced.

The elephants, guided by Oba's telepathic commands, stormed through the enemy ranks, causing chaos and confusion. The rival soldiers, unprepared for this awe-inspiring force, faltered in their attempts to resist. The elephants trampled through their formations, scattering their forces and instilling fear in their hearts.

King Oba, a fierce and strategic leader, capitalized on the moment of disarray. He rallied his troops, inspiring them to fight with unmatched courage and determination. The Benin warriors, armed with spears, shields, and the will to defend their homeland, pushed forward with relentless fervor.

The battle raged on, but the elephants, with their sheer size and strength became the defining factor in Oba's victory. Their tremendous power, combined with the strategic genius of King Oba, overwhelmed King Adeolu's forces, forcing them into retreat.

Word of King Oba's triumph spread far and wide, solidifying his reputation as a formidable ruler and warrior. The tale of the battle, with elephants charging into the fray under the guidance of their king, echoed through the generations, becoming a cherished part of Benin's folklore.

Now let us carefully examine the details. As a reminder, It's necessary to understand that war is deception, deflection, and deterrence. The details in folklore or just as variable as details in historical documents, are capable of being manipulated to discourage or insinuate thought processes of the mind. Let's deal with the folklore and tell her the elephants, as it is known to have elephants in the area and it is more likely to be true than it is not to be true but in war numbers are

exaggerated and capabilities exaggerated meant to create an illusion to instill fear. Whether it be one elephant or 10 or anthropomorphize an army of soldiers as to be literal elephants is not a stretch. And figuratively speaking, the destructive power of elephants is embodied in a warring army.

So whether it could be taken to be figurative or literal, as an adversary if one heard that an opposing kingdom had 50,000 elephants trained and mounted for destruction and it to be known that there are trained elephants present, one could perceive that's possibly a reality to there being 50,000 ready war elephants. In any case, those kinds of numbers in the ancient world would not Be a kingdom to provoke If you had no solid proof. So to see 30 or 40 trained elephants in tribal cultural regalia and prepared for war, you could suppose it to be true if the area is populated with thousands of free-roaming elephants at their disposal. So with this thought it should be clear That war is in the mind first.
And it starts with a tale or folklore.

According to globally accepted sources of documents and religious texts, the Bible is accepted as historical. And there are poor principles that we will address. Cultures around the world have a variation of the flood story but in any case, we Will only address what is accepted literature for the areas of discussion. Babylon, Egypt, and Ethiopia. We could address Canaan and the Horn of Africa and Arabia but these are encapsulated as the region itself. And in the region itself, it is accepted as truth that the three main relatives of one ancestor who survived a flood with his family? The main families recognized in the region are Egypt, Ethiopia, and Babylon. And the sons' names were Shem Khem and Yapeth. As an

agreed upon ancestor for all three to be brothers and sons of the father Noah.

The name Noah may vary from coach to culture but it is accepted that he built a ship and he also commanded animals of every kind. If we decide to look at this text and interpret it without any religious bias and to accept it as a cultural, historical, and ancestral story, the story says that the founders of Egypt Ethiopia, and Babylon were Great ancestors who were seafarers and trained all animals in the world today and all the animals taming that exists today began our ancestor and the origin of civilization by him. As a reference, there are hieroglyphs in Egypt of the Egyptians trading with the animals as we stated in the earlier chapters that they traded and trained all the animals of the land.

"1880 exotic animals brought back to African market"

The rhino, the elephant, the giraffe, the bullocks, the crocodiles, we see all in the hieroglyphs. And specifically, the key point is that they're trading in the young calves and offspring of the livestock. It is and should be common sense that the main timing of animals is by way of food and early presence. Early presents, preferably at birth. And the book of

Joshua gives an illustration of the young animals coming to the ark and not full-size adults. Jasher 6: 3-9

And the Lord brought this about on the next day, and animals, beasts, and fowls came in great multitudes and surrounded the ark.

And Noah went and seated himself by the door of the ark, and of all flesh that crouched before him, he brought into the ark, and all that stood before him he left upon earth.

And a lioness came, with her two whelps, male and female, and the three crouched before Noah, and the two whelps rose against the lioness and smote her, and made her flee from her place, and she went away, and they returned to their places, and crouched upon the earth before Noah.

And the lioness ran away and stood in the place of the lions.

And Noah saw this, and wondered greatly, and he rose and took the two whelps, and brought them into the ark.

And Noah brought into the ark from all living creatures that were upon earth, so that there was none left but which Noah brought into the ark.

Two and two came to Noah into the ark, but from the clean animals, and clean fowls, he brought seven couples, as God had commanded him.

And all the animals, beasts, and fowls were still there, and they surrounded the ark at every place, and the rain had not descended till seven days after."

It's common sense that training and timing begin with a young person.

Mali

In the case of Mali, This is where the plot thickens, It is rumored and asserted that the English translations omitted great offenses. In the literal intentional misrepresentation and altering of script and translation. This is why we have alternating descriptions of the information and recitation according to different scholars, and by no means she would misunderstand that most scholars and or members of royal courts or or delegates played multiple roles as spies and ambassadors. Which military information and military assets were and still are valuable information. This will be addressed immediately after exert.

In the work of al-Hasan Ibn Muhammad Ibn Ahmad al-Wazzan descriptions of Africa. He speaks about Mensa Suleiman, the sultan of Mali at that time. If indeed the literal text is replaced.
It would read as follows…

"The royal court is magnificent and very well organized. When the king goes from one city to another with the members of his court, he rides a camel (elephant), and the horses are led by hand by servants.
If fighting becomes necessary, the servants mount the camels(elephants), and all the soldiers mount the horses."

Exert Kingdom of Mali

"This kingdom (11) extends along one of the branches of the Niger for a distance of about three hundred miles, bordering the former kingdom

from the north, and wilderness with rugged mountains from the south, bordered to the west by deserted ends extending to the ocean, and the east by the Kago region. And in this country, there is a great village containing about six thousand canons, and it is called Mali (12), and it gave its name to the rest of the kingdom. It is inhabited by the king and his entourage, and grain, meat, and cotton abound in the country. There are in this village a large number of resident and casual artisans and merchants, to whom the king pays more attention than others, and the inhabitants are rich thanks to their trade, as they supply Guinea and Timbuktu with many products. And they have many mosques and imams and professors who teach in mosques"

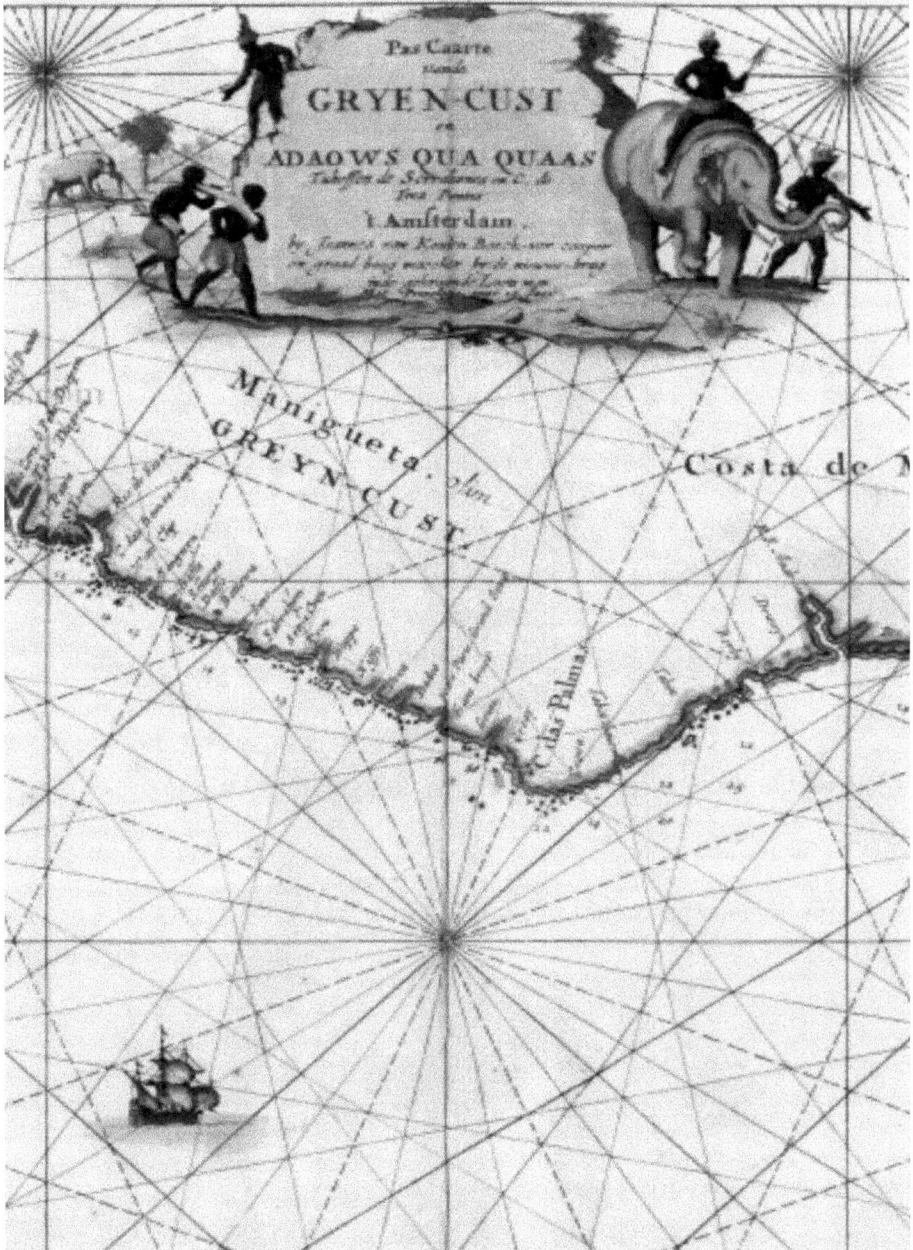

Map of the Grain Coast - the western coast of the Gulf of Guinea, oriented to the North

1683

Title: Pas Caarte vande Gryen-Cust en Adaows qua Quaas tuhessen de Serraliones en C. de Tres Puntas.'t Amsterdam | by Joannes van Keulen Boeck-ver cooper en graad boog maecker by de nieuwe-brug inde gekroonde Loots man.

Met Privilegie voor 15 Jaar.

Area all incompassing Mali Songhai Ghana Benin

It was originally written by Ali, as well as by Al-Saadi and other Sudanese historians, and it is the great kingdom that the Mandingo people formed and reached the height of its greatness in the ninth century" Hijri / 14 AD.

See: Details of the Kingdom of Mali according to Abd al-Qadir Ziyadiyah, The Kingdom of Salafi, p. 12, and later on

The matter may be related to Niani, a village on Shahr Sankarani near Al-Taqala

in Niger. The capital of Mali has been moved several times.

1815 ArtistGrangerMediumPainting DescriptionABOLITION OF
SLAVERY, 1815. English officer telling Africans of the abolition of
slavery under the Treaty of Peace of 20 September 1815.

This next exert is from the travels of Evliya in the journeys of the Nile
again in relation to the connected societies and cross the border

interactions and technology and skills expressing this sub-Saharan prehistoric training of elephants to be across the continent.

Exert
Evliya Çelebi Travels

"The reason this fortress is called Kanisa ('Church') is that three hours west of here, in a pleasant and airy plain, is the Friday Mosque of the Prophet Solomon, which is constructed like a church, with its prayer-niche facing north towards Jerusalem. Thus this ancient mosque was called Kanisa, and the fortress was named after the mosque. [Elaborate description of the mosque' with 1,700 porphyry columns, etc.]

Y407a [...] Y407b [...] If this mosque were in a civilised country it would be a paradise; but it is an orphaned mosque, without a congregation. It is, however, the site of an annual gathering in the autumn season, when myriads of people from throughout the African continent set up their tents in and near the mosque and around the nearby lake and have a lively open-air market for 40 days and 40 nights. This large lake has a circumference of 11 stages. All these people camp on both sides of the lake and drink its water for a blessing, saying that it is water that was drunk by the Prophet Solomon; and by God's command, those afflicted with various illnesses are cured. At the end of 40 days, when the market is over, countless elephants and camels and donkeys are loaded with skins and pots full of the life-giving water of this lake, which are taken throughout Christendom (kafiristan) and the Arab world. Not a drop of water is left in this lake, which has a circumference of 17 stages. By the following year, however, it is full to the brim, by God's command. It is a great marvel. And it is a great mosque of light, whose servants and scholars Y408a shut the 40 doors constructed of yellow brass and tin and

busy themselves with the religious sciences. The people are all Malikis.
[...]"

Our journey of recital has reached the mythical land, the land of gold in the land of kings of wealth and told, the Empire of Mali, born out of a rich indigenous ancestry and I'm spanning through history to what is no doubt a powerhouse of the land of Kings. The Western royalty and the Eastern royalty of Africa combined giving rise to who is known to be the richest man to ever live and whose ancestry is at the foundation of the exploration of the Atlantic Ocean. Amazingly, we will backtrack to the Ethiopian Axumite Empire to begin our expedition. But first, we will lay the foundation by the source we use as our understanding which is the same source of description of Ghana that will apply to The empire of Mali as our climax to the Western African empires utilizing the African scholar Leo Africanus. The importance of Leo Africanus is his travels first hand that also led to other scholars quoting his work but him as the source being born in Al Andalus, Muslim, Spain. And having lived in Fez, Morocco. The importance of his mentioned at this point is that of language, the language that stretches through to survival this very day to which it is Arabic, and in such a way that the manipulation of translations is easily spotted and the perpetual use of redefining ideas by way of intentional false translations.

"The ethnicities, kingdoms, and empires of Kush, Khemite, Carthage, Axum, Kemem, Bornu, Mauritanian, Libyan, Ghana, Mali, Nigerian, Congolese, Punt, Somalian, Horn African, and Koi San-related peoples of the South represent the genetic makeup of the ancient Kushite Empire, as well as the genetic diversity in the northwest and south regions of the African continent, along with various kingdoms.

Within each of these regions, diverse African ethnicities formed the foundation of clan-based tribal and skill-based systems of ancestral trades

and skills. Ancestral lineages played a pivotal role in determining one's societal responsibilities based on the lineage to which they were born. This division gave rise to distinct tribes specializing in various tasks, including those responsible for middle work, weapon crafting, animal training for war and food, shipbuilding, ship sales, royalty, religion, and priesthood.

These divisions find parallels in the Bible, where Moses allocated specific tasks to each tribe during the construction of the Tabernacle, defining their roles and contributions." This is the most distinct indication of early Kushite systems of civilizations that are mentioned in the Bible after the African kingdom of Khemite Mizraim/ Egypt collapsed. The writers of the Bible identify that the Israelite nation of Hebrew people was formed after the collapse of the Egyptian Empire after being part of the early related lineages of Egypt 400 years ago as a group of people and years before the injury of their foundational tribal group of 70 Hebrew people. Beginning with the book of Exodus chapter 35 gives the illustrations of the different clans that Moses instructed to be the skillet workers of the specific skills. Such Levi: The tribe of Levi was primarily responsible for the priestly duties, including the construction of the Tabernacle itself, as well as the associated rituals and offerings. Aaron and his sons, from the tribe of Levi, served as priests.

Judah: Bezalel, who was from the tribe of Judah, was chosen to lead the skilled craftsmen in the construction of various items for the Tabernacle, such as the Ark of the Covenant.

Dan: Oholiab, from the tribe of Dan, was selected to work alongside Bezalel and assist in the skilled craftsmanship required for the construction of the tabernacle and its furnishings.

Bezalel and Oholiab: These individuals, chosen by God, were filled with the Spirit of God and had the skills for various forms of craftsmanship, including metalworking. Bezalel, from the tribe of Judah, played a prominent role in overseeing the construction of items like the Ark of the Covenant (Exodus 31:1-5).

Levi: While the Levites were primarily responsible for priestly duties, they also played roles in constructing and maintaining the Tabernacle. This could have included tasks related to metalwork as part of their broader responsibilities.

Artisans and Craftsmen: Exodus 35:30-35 mentions "every skilled person whom the Lord has given skill and ability" who was responsible for various crafts, including metalwork. These individuals came from among the Israelites as a whole, not necessarily from specific tribes. So then in these very instances, we see the ancient societal structures of clan-based contributions. Rather than prolong the information, we will concisely address the matter before we move any further, here and now let us begin.

In many ways, this created job security as well as pricing and status. However, according to some aspects, the more lucrative trades were more subject to deceptions and betrayals and would oftentimes and could oftentimes lead to the overthrow or demise of a kingdom in itself. If not, probably managed. Some of these skill-based trade secrets are geography,

ship making, and Corsair's. The sailors and semen warriors of nations battled on these high seas and imported trade from the seas.

To be briefed on this point we will say oftentimes many of these explorer trade skills resulted in false information, protecting trade routes on the land and trade routes of the sea with stories of horror and great beasts to deter others from seeking out and finding faraway lands and distances that presented great wealth and opportunities. We still find this today in modern society with demonizations of locations and regions of the world where there is very low value to the resources to where those who can reach them can get them at slave prices while those in the faraway land of the imports are scared or feared and told to stay away, while the propheteers profit lavishly the immense wealth being held the secret by tales of goblins and folklore. We have seen this in ancient times in the tales of Carthage and their travels up and down the west coast of Africa and the trade of the Phoenicians all across Africa but they remained very tight-knit. Just as trade secrets in today's society. The civilizations of the past is where it all started with clan base knowledge and secrecy with heavy misdirective misinformation.

There were no more secretive clans than those of royalty, priesthood, metalworking, animal training, and medicine. The voyages believed to have been taken by the Phoenicians across the globe in the early years of the Empire and civilizations by sea have been debated in many circles due to evidence that seems to be out of place. Regarding mainstream history, for instance, this example wants to be established.
We will return to the issue of the clans but first, the Phoenicians although it may seem out of place in this segment is relative to the matter.

In 1872, a stone inscribed with Phoenician writing was allegedly discovered in Paraíba, Brazil. It tells of a Phoenician ship that was separated from a fleet sailing from Egypt around Africa, and it mentions the pharaoh Necho I or Necho II.

During the time frame of approximately 1400 BCE to 400 BCE, which is roughly the period of the Olmec civilization in the Americas, the pharaohs of Egypt changed over time due to the dynastic history of ancient Egypt. Here are some of the notable pharaohs and periods during that time:

New Kingdom (c. 1550–1070 BCE): This era includes prominent pharaohs like Thutmose III (ruled c. 1479–1425 BCE),

Amenhotep III (ruled c. 1386–1353 BCE), Akhenaten (ruled c. 1353–1336 BCE), and Tutankhamun (ruled c. 1332–1323 BCE).

Late Period (c. 664–332 BCE): During this time, notable pharaohs include Necho II (ruled c. 610–595 BCE), Psammetichus I (ruled c. 664–610 BCE), and others. It's worth noting that this period also saw the influence of foreign rulers, such as the Persians.

Ptolemaic Period (c. 332–30 BCE): Following the conquest of Egypt by Alexander the Great and the establishment of the Ptolemaic dynasty, notable pharaohs include Ptolemy I Soter (ruled c. 305–283 BCE) and Cleopatra VII (ruled c. 51–30 BCE).

While the Olmec civilization was flourishing in the Americas and the dynastic history of Egypt was evolving, the alleged Phoenician inscription in Brazil suggests a potential connection or exploration between Phoenician sailors and the American continent. However, this claim remains a subject of historical debate and scrutiny within the academic community, and concrete evidence supporting such transoceanic voyages is still under evaluation.

West Africa, which is usually identified with Carthage (located in modern-day Tunisia) on the Mediterranean coast:

Phoenicians (c. 1550–332 BCE):
The Phoenician civilization is known to have emerged around 1550 BCE. Phoenician city-states like Tyre, Sidon, and Byblos were established along the eastern Mediterranean coast.
Phoenician maritime trade and exploration played a significant role in the Mediterranean region during this time, with Carthage being one of their westernmost trade posts on the Atlantic coast of North Africa.

Egyptian New Kingdom (c. 1550–1070 BCE):
Prominent pharaohs of the New Kingdom, including Thutmose III and Amenhotep III, ruled during this period.
The Egyptian empire reached its zenith, expanding its influence in the region.
Olmec Civilization (c. 1400–400 BCE):
The Olmec civilization in the Americas was thriving during this time, known for its art and monumental sculptures.

Late Period Egypt (c. 664–332 BCE):
During this period, Egypt saw the influence of foreign powers, including the Assyrians and Persians.

Phoenician Voyages and Trade (Throughout):
The Phoenicians were renowned sailors and traders throughout this time frame, establishing colonies and trade networks in various Mediterranean regions.

Their westernmost Atlantic trade post was Carthage, located on the Mediterranean coast of North Africa (modern-day Tunisia).

Please note that Carthage, while considered a Phoenician colony, was not on the Atlantic coast of West Africa but rather on the Mediterranean coast, as the Phoenicians did not establish colonies along the Atlantic coast of West Africa as far as Morocco. This information is relative at this point in establishing the societal norms of the era of civilization where nations were skilled-based and clan-based and the connecting point of these errors to the historical text of the Hebrew Bible with a dimension of the pharaoh Neko as during these times the Phoenicians as a semitic people or also intertwined with the legacies of the Western Semitic peoples and the Mediterranean as a whole as Afroasiatic people groups in complete control of global navigation of the seas. Necho II is highly likely to be the same Pharaoh Neco referenced in the Bible's 2 Kings, 2 Chronicles, and Jeremiah. His second campaign aimed at conquering Asia and halting the westward expansion of the Neo-Babylonian Empire while disrupting its trade route over the Euphrates River. Having delved into the tales of origin, let us now navigate towards the primary issue."

That first glance recombining all of the ethnicities of the royal African war elephant and the widely spread practice of taming and training beats of burden and war throughout the continent north, south-east and west, not only by the movement of people carrying culture and traditions in migrations throughout trade in the empires of the continent, here are the listings of now existing ethnicities related to the regions of the once held territories of African Empires.

Clans from East to West   North and South Most commonly renowned for their animal husbandry and training and timing Warrior status.

Maasai
Fulani (Fula)
Tuareg
Himba
Nuer
Oromo Barabaig
Dinka
Bakwena
Amhara
Yoruba
Zulu
Khoisan (San)
Dogon (Mali)
Somali
Afar
Tigray
Argobba
Harla
Kuba
Luba
Mbuti
Beja
Teke

Keeping in mind that in the loss of battles and empires, as we concluded earlier, comes the loss of technologies, skills, and personnel that parish with tightly knit societies of ancestral clan and tribal structures that held the secrets well but that same strength also manifests itself as a weakness in loss. Also really illustrates the tribal clan structures of not only animal husbandry and specific skills, but the empire of Mali is well documented as well as Ghana. Well documented to manage and secrecy of trade routes and locations of deposits of gold and trade secrets to maintain hegemony in specific sectors of trade and commerce.

The Mali Empire from the 13th to the 17th century. It was located in what is now Mali, Senegal, Gambia, Guinea, Mauritania, and parts of Niger and Burkina Faso. The empire was founded by Sundiata Keita, a legendary warrior king, in 1230. 1230: Sundiata Keita, also known as the Lion King, establishes the Mali Empire after defeating the Sosso Empire in the Battle of Kirina.

1235-1255: Sundiata Keita expands the Mali Empire through conquest, gaining control over the gold and salt trade routes and establishing a capital at Niani.

1307: Mansa Musa becomes king of the Mali Empire, ushering in a period of great prosperity and expansion.

1324: Mansa Musa embarks on a pilgrimage to Mecca, bringing with him a large entourage and vast amounts of gold. His pilgrimage earns him fame throughout the Islamic world and establishes Mali as a major center of trade and scholarship.

1337-1374: Reign of Mansa Suleyman, who continues the expansion of the Mali Empire and establishes Timbuktu as a center of Islamic scholarship and learning.

1380: Mali begins to decline after the death of Mansa Suleyman. Internal conflicts, rebellions, and attacks by neighboring states weaken the empire.

1464-1492: Reign of Sunni Ali Ber, founder of the Songhai Empire, which eventually conquers and absorbs the Mali Empire.

1591: The Moroccan invasion of the Songhai Empire marks the end of the Mali Empire and the beginning of the era of European colonialism in West Africa.

Malian Proverb

"Salt comes from the north, gold from the south, but the word of God and the treasures of wisdom are only to be found in Timbuktu." Timbuktu and its zenith and its glory, was the largest center of learning in the world. And all of the world's leading fields of education were primarily centered in Timbuktu, including animal husbandry.

" Mansa Musa was a devout Muslim and observed one of the five pillars of Islam by undertaking a pilgrimage to Mecca (known as Hajj). When he embarked on his Hajj in 1324, he traveled thousands of miles across treacherous terrain with 60,000 people, 21,000 kilograms of gold, 100 elephants, and 80 camels" bbc.co.uk

And now to Bilal… At the heart of this narrative lies an unshakable truth - the proud lineage of Mansa Musa and his predecessor trace their origin to the legendary Bilal. Who was Bilal? He was not merely a name etched in history; he was the living embodiment of resilience and courage. His father's name was Rabah, and his mother, a Hebrew Jewish woman, was captured during the fateful Year of the Elephant and thrust into the chains

of slavery. From the land of Habesha, modern-day Ethiopia, Bilal emerged his very existence an anthem of strength and endurance.

Attributes adorned Bilal, making him an indomitable force in the conversion to Islam. His voice resonated not just in sound but in power - the first muezzin, a herald of the faith, summoning believers to prayer. His unwavering faith reverberated through the ages, a testament to the foundations of Islam. His dominance was not born of brute strength alone; it was a presence felt in the conviction of his beliefs, an unyielding spirit that forged the bedrock of his legacy.

Descendants of Bilal Who are the illustrious Keita clan became vast in numbers, in the journey of migration to West Africa, Mali thriving in their blood, and Jewish ancestry coursed through their veins, an unbreakable thread woven by Bilal's mother. Their melding with the Mandinka people cemented a heritage defined by diversity and strength.

Islam's stories and the echoes of war elephants offered them power, a power that found its zenith in the legacy of Mansa Musa. With wealth unmeasurable and a heart unburdened by the trivial, Mansa Musa's reign was the very embodiment of opulence. He traversed lands, leaving his footsteps imprinted in the annals of history, the richest man to ever grace the Earth. In his wake, he left a throne, not as a mere artifact of power, but as a testament to a legacy that would forever resonate.

And in the tempest of the Atlantic's expanse, a journey set sail, led by those who bore the lineage of Bilal and the Keita clan. Across the vast unknown, they embarked, setting forth a connection that would transcend continents and epochs. Their journey, a tribute to ancestry, was marked by 200 ships, then 2000, laden with goods and elephants
- symbols of power and majesty. Mansa Musa's predecessor Abu Bakr
, heir to this legacy embarked on a world-shattering expedition across the Atlantic, and Mansa Musa was given the throne, embracing the title of the world's richest, the African sun illuminating his ascent.

In the expanse of time, the Mandinka people, distant relatives of the African Americans, find themselves as stars in the same constellation. The shared ancestry, the echoes of the past, bind them together across oceans and years. It is in this tale that we find the journey of Bilal and the lineage of Mansa Musa as a beacon of unity, their stories speaking not just to the past, but to the unbreakable ties that span generations, peoples, and continents.

West of his kingdom.

Al-Umarirecorded the story Mansa Musa told in Egypt in 1324: "The monarch who preceded me would not believe that it was impossible to discover the limits of the neighboring sea. He wished to know. He persisted in his plan. He caused the equipping of two hundred ships and filled them with men, and of each such number they were filled with gold, water, and food for two years. He said to the commanders: "Do not return until you have reached the end of the ocean, or when you have exhausted your food and water."

According to al-Umari, only one ship returned. Its captain reported to Abubakari that he had watched as the other ships sailed on, entered a broad current in the ocean, and disappeared.

Abubakari then decided to build a fleet of two thousand boats and command it himself. In 1311 Abubakari set out with his fleet down the Senegal River and headed west in the Atlantic. He never returned to Mali, and his brother became Mansa Musa in 1312.

Malian scholar Gaoussou Diawara has argued that he reached the Americas sometime in the early 14th century. Another historian and linguist, Leo Weiner, in his book; Africa and the discovery of America explained how Columbus noted in his journal that Native Americans had confirmed that "black-skinned people had come from the south-east in boats, trading in gold-tipped spears

"Point to remember"

Maps are authentic publications respected worldwide and are used for historical references in terms of location and descriptive depictions. They represent the mindset of a people and an era of that time. Much can be debated, refuted, denied, or even dismissed as legend false or true. But it is and has proven to be widely circulated. Agreed upon knowledge and general descriptions that represent land distance people and culture icons presented and projected.

Also, we should note that In 1970, Thor Heyerdahl and his crew conducted an expedition known as the "Ra II" voyage. They sailed across the Atlantic Ocean from Morocco in North Africa to Barbados in the Caribbean on a reed boat called the Ra II. This voyage aimed to demonstrate the feasibility of transatlantic travel using ancient materials and methods.

Understanding these depictions illustrated in the pre-colonial maps where Mansa Musa the emperor of Mali is oftentimes presented by his depiction on the map that is used to validate and substantiate his presence and representation which is also why other parts of that same map or not widely circulated due to other representations that have now become politically and sociologically rejected and refuted for socioeconomic and psychological purposes of a mindset formulated created that benefited blocking visuals of dominating African military force to be replaced with those of race represented subjugation and despair.

It is reasonable to conclude that given Timbuktu's central role in education encompassing fields like geometry, mathematics, husbandry, and various forms of knowledge, including sacred texts, maps, and navigation history, there was abundant information and expertise available. When considering that Mansa Musa's predecessor reportedly

embarked on a voyage with a fleet of 2,000 ships and modern evidence suggesting that one could navigate from the west coast of Africa to the Americas using reed ships and the West African sea current, it becomes increasingly likely, if not unquestionable, that knowledge of navigation, ship construction, and the training of elephants was not only feasible but well-established in this region.

Where are the relative elephant regalia pieces? The elephant tus blades the elephant headdressed the elephant thrones the elephant saddles the elephant armors the elephant towers the elephant national fabrics of Kush, Egypt, Mali of Zulu of Benin I was Zimbabwe of Ethiopia. Where is the regalia? Who has it and what museums a public or a museum are stored away deep in the halls of billionaire private museums, one of a kind with rare items never before photographed. Where are they?

Yes, we know much is destroyed in war just as much as is taken but not only taken, also lost in the souls of those who carry the knowledge and the histories and the skills with them into the afterlife. As we stated before that the secrecies of clans for the purpose of security that gets destroyed when those who carry the secrets parish, there should still be ample evidences that remain because of the characteristics of kings to desire a trophies. And to end this segment of Islam with the highlight of the black Sultan of Sudan.

Ottomans archives. In 1673 *Sudan Sultanate* 2,000 *elephants*.

" Ottoman exploration of the Nile" 1670
Travelogger geographer "Evliya Celebi"

"Continuing south along the Nile, we passed through several prosperous vil- lages and in ten hours arrived at the City of Borushesh. Y423a A qan who is the Sultan of Sudan's vizier governs here over 100,000 troops, 2,000 elephants, 500,000 subjects and countless animals. He came out to greet the sultan with all kinds of creatures God be praised, None shall question Him about His works (Qur'an 21:23). And what sorts of human beings He has created! How can hearing measure up to seeing? When this vizier came out to greet us, he brought two enormous elephants, one of them as white as milk and 1,000 years old, or so they told us. They could only be mounted with a rope ladder of 20 rungs. I had never seen such huge elephants. And they were very tame and docile, following a man like a dog for a scrap of bread. But they were not voracious like the elephants in Ottoman lands, though they had grown pleasantly plump from catching the breeze. And they were enamoured of people. What happened was that the thi noceros of Dervish Ni'metullâh, our companion from Qal'at Itshan, when it saw those elephants, started to attack them and Dervish Ni metullah had a hard time controlling it. And when the elephants saw the rhinoceros, they became restless and began picking up sticks and the like from the ground and spewing them in the air and trumpeting with a melancholy voice like that of a virgin girl. Each elephant was mounted by 40 lovely Baghanisqi mamluks. Such were the gifts brought to the king.

Departing from Borushesh, we went another seven hours south along the Nile to the Stage of Qal'at Boruste, the City of Ibristan ('The Hebrew Country').

"This is the concept and future of African museums built by Africans"

DE L'AFRIQUE. 125

FIGURE XLVIII.

Elefans " (De L'Afrique)

1685 African M'banza-Kongo São Salvador Kongo 17th Century
Print Mallet

These proofs of descriptions of civilization on the continent of
Africa are of the most profound importance to the restoration of the
raw African war elephant in history represented by African people.
Every illustration and depiction has been pre-colonial during the
times of autonomy and sovereignty of African kingdoms.

Chapter 7
Kingdom of Kongo

African Proverb;
"The elephant's tusks never become a burden to him"

We now highlight the Kongo Empire. The Kingdom of Kongo is everything Africa is made of. The vast open African jungle teeming with life. Endless mountain ranges and flowing rivers tamed and untamed beasts of all sizes in the Splenda and beauty Africa as well as the fear. Pinnacle of this edition of the African War Elephant. The Grand Kingdom of Kongo is a bustling trade hub of every surrounding kingdom from African geography. The most feared African warrior inhabiting and mastering the true jungle. The forging of weaponry was created to strike fear at the very site of the iron smelting metalwork. The Great Kingdom of Kongo.

To the great warriors of the Kongo who traversed mountain trained and handled the mighty Kong War Element, which was the inspiration for the depictions of Kongo War Elephant. Salute

you with honor as little is known of who you were or your native stories or battles You want a loss? The honor we give you is one of. Thanks to whatever season or time you were seen mountain on your fellow companions training or patrolling the areas that gave the inspiration for the depiction and description of Congo war elephants. We thank you and we think of the elephants to whom we know not their names, nor their stories but we think of them also or the patients and compliance with you our fellow Africans. This illustration and depiction is therefore the foundation created. Build a tribute and display mounted. African elephants have a fact of history mounted by African warriors wielding weapons in tribal headdress training patrolling and representing The now ancient African power of the Royal African war elephant.

"Additionally"

A point to remember and connection with this is of the greatest importance to remember that each one of these illustrations that depictions whether on the map or the specific depiction of El Salvador Congo and the illustration of the Zara people of the River Niger is this point that the sub-Saharan taming training and representation of war elephants are documented. pre-Belgium pre-British dominance to the Niger River region as a documented description of the civilizations not only hunting the elephant but to mount them as well. This one Congo depiction alone is the dismissal of any discredit and evidence as to why the images are not widely circulated although for those trained in history and cartography and European illustrations of Africa or well aware of these illustrations although it can be understood that people not of

the discriminated race to have any desire of eradicate the myths with these illustrations. The one would think it would be an honest duty, it is understood not to be their responsibility but the responsibility, of the people to whom it affects negatively restorative."

The oral traditions of the Congo people are rich with diverse origin stories that reflect the cultural complexity and uniqueness of the region. These stories vary among different tribes and communities, each contributing its narrative to the tapestry of Congo's history. While I can't provide an exhaustive list, I can offer a glimpse into a few notable origin stories:

Kuba Kingdom's Origin Story: The Kuba people of the Democratic Republic of Congo have an origin story that revolves around Woot, the mythical founding ancestor. According to their oral tradition, Woot descended from the heavens to establish the Kuba Kingdom. He brought with him the royal symbols, including the drum and the leopard, which holds great significance in Kuba culture. This origin narrative underscores the importance of ancestral connections and the divine nature of the kingdom's founding.

Africa
José Theophilo (Theóphilo, Teofilo) de Jesus
Description
Brazilian painter1758 -1847

Luba-Lunda Origin Story: The Luba and Lunda people of the central Congo region share a legend that traces their lineage to a single ancestor, Kalala Ilunga. The story tells of a journey across

vast lands, with each of his sons becoming the founder of different Luba and Lunda chiefdoms. This narrative highlights the interconnectedness of the Luba and Lunda tribes, as well as the significance of lineage and ancestral ties.

Bakongo Creation Myth: The Bakongo people's oral tradition includes a creation myth that involves the deity Nzambi Mpungu. In this narrative, Nzambi Mpungu shaped the world and humanity. His creation of humans involved sculpting clay figures and breathing life into them. This story encapsulates the Bakongo's spiritual beliefs and underscores the divine connection between the creator and his creation.

Teke People's Origins: The Teke people's origin story speaks of a migration journey from a distant land. They believe their ancestorsb traversed a great distance and overcame challenges to reach their current homeland. The tale highlights the Teke people's historical migrations and their resilience in the face of adversity. Bambuti People's Creation Story: The Bambuti, often referred to as Pygmies, have their own creation story. They believe that the creator deity shaped the first humans from clay and then breathed life into them. The Bambuti emphasize their harmonious relationship with the forest and their deep connection to the natural world.

These origin stories, along with many others of Kongo's diverse cultures are the treasures of Africa. They provide insight into how different tribes perceive their origins, relationships with the land, and connections to the spiritual realm. The oral traditions of the

Kongo people serve as repositories of wisdom, history, and identity, passed down through generations as a testament to the richness of this region's cultural heritage. Listing all the kings of the Congo, along with the years of their rule and their tribes, is a complex task due to the extensive history of the region and the limited available historical records. However, I can provide you with a list of some of the notable kings from the Kingdom of Kongo, along with the approximate years of their reigns and their tribes:

1. **Lukeni lua Nimi (Late 14th century):** Believed to be the founder of the Kongo Kingdom. Tribe: Bakongo.

Nzinga a Nkuwu (circa 1470–1509): Also known as João I of Kongo. Tribe: Bakongo.

. **Alfonso I (1509–1543):** Also known as Afonso I. Tribe: Bakongo.

Diogo I (1545–1561): Also known as Diogo I Mpanzu. Tribe: Bakongo.

Alvare I (1561–1567): Also known as Álvaro I. Tribe: Bakongo. nga. Tribe: Bakongo.
Many more kings ruled the Kongo Kingdom and other regions in the Kongo. **Bernardo I (1567–1571):** Also known as Bernardo I Nimi a Lukeni. Tribe: Bakongo.

Henrique I (1571–1592): Also kno]'

\wn as Henrique I Nkanga a Lukeni. Tribe: Bakongo.

Alvare II (1595–1614): Also known as Álvaro II. Tribe:

Bakongo.

Bernardo II (1614–1622): Also known as Bernardo II Mbemba a Nkanga. Tribe: Bakongo.

. **Alvare III (1622–1624):** Also known as Álvaro III. Tribe: Bakongo.

Pedro II (1624–1626): Also known as Pedro II Nkanga a Lukeni.
Tribe: Bakongo.

Alvare IV (1626–1636): Also known as Álvaro IV. Tribe: Bakongo.

Bernardo III (1636–1641): Also known as Bernardo III Mbemba a Nkanga. Tribe: Bakongo.

Pedro III (1641–1661): Also known as Pedro III a Nkanga. Tribe: Bakongo.

Alvare V (1661–1665): Also known as Álvaro V. Tribe: Bakongo.

Antonio I (1665–1669): Also known as António I. Tribe: Bakongo.

Pedro IV (1669–1718): Also known as Pedro IV a Nkanga. Tribe: Bakongo.

Garcia II (1743–1746): Also known as Garcia II Nkanga a Lukeni. Tribe: Bakongo.

Alvare VI (1746–1752): Also known as Álvaro VI. Tribe: Bakongo.

Henrique II (1765–1766): Also known as Henrique II a Nka

The Congo Empire was a bustling trade hub with numerous powerful kingdoms and regions, fostering trade connections that spanned Ghana, Mali, Ethiopia, the Sahara, Morocco, Arabia, Zimbabwe, and other central and western African kingdoms. This developed and fortified powerhouse possessed impressive military might and weaponry, with its legendary elephants renowned throughout the entirety of Africa, earning the epithet " the elephant never gets tired of his tusks." The 1685 illustration of the S. Salvador trade vividly depicted this network of commerce and the remarkable role of these mighty elephants in the heart of the Kongo's trade relationships.

DE L'AFRIQUE. 127

FIGURE XLIX.

"Elefans " (De L'Afrique) Mallet, Allain Manesson Publication Date: 1683"

"Depiction of several African warriors in tribal, headdress and armed with spears and training with elephants, one kneeling, one performing maneuvers, one mounted and another grazing "

In the heart of the African continent, amidst lush landscapes and winding river valleys, emerges the awe-inspiring origin story of the Kongo. This tale unfolds with the resonance of ancient drum beats, echoing through time, tracing back to a time of Bantu migrations that cast destiny's death.

From the distant horizons of history, the tribes of the Kongo arose like constellations in the night sky, their diverse cultures glimmering with unique brilliance. Among them, the Bakongo tribe stood as pillars of strength, their spirit intertwined with the very soil they tread. Their footprints marked the path towards a collective destiny, each tribe nurturing its customs, tales, and languages like precious gems.

Amidst the undulating hills and verdant plains, the Kongo Kingdom was woven into existence. Lukeni lua Nimi, a legendary figure, carved the first lines of this saga, casting the cornerstone of a realm destined to flourish. His footsteps marked the beginning of an epic legacy, one that would stretch through the ages.

As generations unfurled, the Kongo Kingdom burgeoned, its borders expanding with the weight of ambition. Kings rose like towering baobabs, their rule synonymous with strength and wisdom. Nzinga a Nkuwu, a ruler of magnanimous vision, navigated through the intricate tides of change, fostering trade winds that carried whispered tales from distant shores. Alfonso I, his successor, stood as an emblem of leadership, bridging cultures, and embracing the dawning light of European contact.

In the shadows of power, tribal clashes and territorial disputes became the undercurrents of this tale. The Luba and Lunda tribes, ensconced in the eastern reaches, charted their narratives of conquest and expansion. Their kings, like luminous stars, guided them through the complexities of history's labyrinth. Battles rumbled across the canvas of the Kongo's landscape, both majestic and harrowing. Wars danced beneath the emerald canopies, each skirmish echoing through the dense forests like thunderclaps. And

amid these struggles emerged a marvel: war elephants, majestic giants that wove both terror and awe. Trained, tamed, and brought to the fore, these creatures bore witness to the ferocity and strategic brilliance that marked these conflicts.

Yet, as the sun reached its zenith, the Congo's fate took an unforeseen turn. The colonial era cast a long shadow over the land, as European powers cast covetous eyes upon its riches. With the machinations of politics and power, the kingdoms fell, and their sovereignty crumbled like ancient ruins under the weight of history.

The origin story of the Congo is a symphony of tribal voices, a mosaic of kings and cultures entwined in a tapestry that stretches across time. It is a tale of resilience, as tribes forged their identities against the backdrop of adversity. It is a chronicle of enlightenment, where the gleam of knowledge illuminated the path through darkness. And even as colonialism cast its pall, the spirit of the Congo remained, a phoenix poised to rise once more, reclaiming its majesty and legacy in the embrace of a new dawn.

"Point to remember"

Let me reiterate once again that these illustrations depicting Africans riding on African elephants in a military formation in cultural headdresses and apparel representing the People of the location in an organized defensive force exist as a fact, and have existed for over 400 years as a fact. Relative to the illustrations of hieroglyphs and artifacts of ancient civilizations and cultures related to the same migrations of people is irrefutable and by

definition prehistoric. As there would be no record to who or from where the first mount was recorded. Logically seeing that all these things were already taking place before Herodotus.... Let me say again that it is worthy to note and I repeat... These illustrations depict Africans writing on African elephants in the military formation and cultural headdresses and weapons representing the people of the location in an organized defensive force exist as fact.

The Kongo Empire is one of the most renowned empires of African history. The Kongo Empire, also known as the Kingdom of Kongo, was powerful and influential. Known not only for the most unique and fear-striking beasts of war, fabled in myths and legends of things unseen in the faraway lands of Europe, the beast's gone extinct due to the changing times of the earth's climate and early man. Trained and trained war elephants, rhinoceroses, hippopotami, horses, zebras, giraffes, bulls, primates, gorillas, and crocodiles all prehistoric. It is renowned for several key aspects of its history and culture. Here are the top five things the Kongo Empire is most renowned for:

Centralized Governance and Social Structure**: The Kingdom of Kongo was known for its well-organized political structure. It had a centralized monarchy with a king, known as the Manikongo, at its head. The kingdom was divided into provinces and had a hierarchical social structure that included nobility, commoners, and slaves.

Trade and Diplomacy: The Kongo Empire was strategically located near the coast, which facilitated trade and diplomatic relations with European powers, particularly during the colonial era. The kingdom engaged in trade with Portuguese explorers and later with other European nations, exchanging goods such as animals, ivory, textiles, and slaves.

Christianity and Cultural Exchange: In the late 15th century, the Kingdom of Kongo became one of the first African regions to adopt Christianity. The reigning king, Nzinga a Nkuwu (King João I), converted to Christianity and was baptized by the Portuguese. This led to a significant cultural exchange between European and Kongo cultures, with the introduction of Christian practices and the establishment of missions.

Ivory and Artistic Achievements: The Congo Empire was renowned for its artistic and cultural achievements. Skilled artisans created intricate sculptures, pottery, and textiles. Ivory carving, in particular, was a significant artistic practice in the kingdom, producing items of great craftsmanship and artistic value.

Collapse and Resistance to Colonialism: The later years of the Congo Empire were marked by challenges and conflicts, including internal strife and external pressures from European colonial powers. The empire's decline was accelerated by the Atlantic slave trade, which significantly weakened the region's population and economy. The Congo people, however, resisted European colonization and sought to maintain their independence and cultural

identity. It's important to note that the history of the Congo Empire is complex, and the details can vary based on historical sources and interpretations. Additionally, the historical narrative may evolve as new research emerges.

Nürnberg bei G. N. Renner & C?

Fr. Friedrich Schwed (pseudonym of Friedrich Schultheiss
1813-1889)

The origin tale of the Kingdom of Kongo commences with the union of Nima a Nzima and Luqueni Luansanze, who was the daughter of Nsa-cu-Clau, the leader of the Mbata people. This marriage solidified an alliance between the Mpemba Kasi and the neighboring Mbata people, forming the very bedrock of the Kingdom of Kongo. From this union, a child named Lukeni lua Nimi was born, destined to become the first to bear the title of Mutinù. Scholars estimate that Lukeni lua Nimi was born between 1367 and 1402 CE. Consequently, historians attribute the establishment of the Kingdom of Kongo to roughly around 1390 CE.

The epicenter of the Kingdom is believed to have emerged in the region of Mpemba Kasi to the south of Kongo. It is thought that Lukeni lua Nimi erected the capital city, Mbanza Kongo. There exists speculation that earlier rulers might have governed a larger expanse before Lukeni lua Nimi's reign, and he, therefore, relocated the capital to that area. During this era, the neighboring Mbata province sought protection and willing submission to the authority of the Kingdom of Kongo. While it is presumed, though not conclusively known, that similar protection pacts existed with other neighboring states of smaller stature. The Kingdom's early formation had a partial basis in conquest, yet it predominantly rested upon voluntary arrangements for protection. With assistance from allied provinces such as Mbete, the Kingdom expanded by conquering Mpangu and Npundi to the south. Appointed governors oversaw these provinces, taking directives from the reigning monarch.

Both Npundi and Mbata proceeded to extend their territories, thereby broadening the borders of the Kingdom of Kongo. By 1490, estimations indicated that the Kingdom boasted a total of about 3 million subjects. It is believed that the Kingdom of Kongo saw six rulers, including Nima a Nzima, despite not assuming the title of King, prior to the year 1490.

This book exists to be a source of reference in the reattribution of the Royal African War elephant in the whole continent of Africa accounting for all the key indigenous African major ethnicities and empires north south east and west as a compilation of illustrations and depictions of the African war elephant in a mounted defensive organized military force culturally distinctive to the people as indigenous Africans pre-colonial and prehistoric. Noting that these published illustrations and depictions respected cartographers and explorers exist as fact, dated titled, and described as Africa.

Many think it involved colonial powers casually marking borders on a map during the 1884 Berlin "The Scramble for Africa" Conference, but the reality is far more complex. The scramble had already commenced prior to the conference, with a crucial stipulation: claimants had to demonstrate effective occupation of a region to legitimize their claims. This sometimes led to intense races between explorers, transcending mere map drawing. Great powers like Britain and France even teetered on the brink of war. Notably, the scramble triggered a revolution in Portugal. Amid this, the narratives of African resistance, barring instances of several

African Kingdoms and Nations, often remain overlooked. Furthermore, the expansion of certain African Kingdoms is frequently omitted. Yet, to comprehend the scramble, delving into history is imperative. Or perhaps not a necessity, but it certainly uncovers captivating empires, wars, and cultural exchanges preceding it. We will revisit the European expansion into Africa further in the next segment.

Initially, the European footholds in Africa were established by the Portuguese as they built bases along their route to India. This spanned from Madeira in the Atlantic to foreign territories like Mozambique, Mombasa, and Zanzibar in East Africa. These strategic points served as vital stopovers for international trade. During this era of colonialism, the standard practice was to set up trade factories and control trade routes rather than seek territorial dominance, owing to their greater profitability. It must be fully understood that none of this could take place without sheer firepower and weaponry. It's proper to keep in mind that the only thing creating the periods of colonialism was the fact that the Industrial Revolution had not yet taken place that manufacture weaponry at high rates of speed. It wasn't morality and religion. It was technology.

A thorough look at the expansion of the Empire during the after the creation of the Gatling gun and rapid-fire weapons and more accurate rifling came the expansion of Europeans' ability to put down the Royal African War Elephants. These battlefield massacres, with all the realities of war, don't make the history books

just as today is history. What happens on the ground does it look good but it is still the realities of war. and in many cases, the real records are for the education of the classified and trained tacticians of war, not for the general public. This would reveal tactics and strategies as well as weaknesses and strong points, and this is the hard reality. As well as the reason why within American society there is a time before information and records can be declassified to give a proper amount of time for those involved as well as all means of threat or liability are mitigated.

One major key point to remember in regards to ethnicity and history, especially in terms of ethnicity because in reality group labels are irrelevant because identity is based solely on ancestry and self-identity. And this is to say this, in research and travel. You see the war elephant statues in regards to those of Rome and early North Africa and Egypt, you will notice that all the figures that control the war elephants are that of an African phenotype, to say a black person, of African descent, but in arguing that same term for ethnicity is irrelevant. Why, because the term negro or African as a whole specific group of phenotypes did not exist at that time. Although terms were used such as Niger, or more, or necro which are Greek and Roman Latin terms, even the term barbarian as far as even the African coast of North Africa was considered The Barbary Coast. But to argue that as an ethnicity in relation to the handlers, one will be refuted without specifics of ethnicity or region which the confusion is created by design. One cannot argue.

The handler is a negro one cannot argue that the handler is an African one. One cannot argue that the handler is black, one cannot argue that the handler is any ethnicity or term that cannot be validated. Conclusively. So in that one must blame the entire loss of African history on the invasions of the Greeks the invasions of the Arabs to the invasions of the Europeans with an intent to divide and conquer and that is just plain history, which is why you cannot argue history in the English based on the spelling of words, but rather the phonetic sound which the very word phonetic is derived from the Phoenician. With this we will examine the sounds of the word war elephant in the world's most prominent language groups. Because language tells a story just as strongly as blood tells a story.

There are hundreds of Bantu languages and several Khoisan languages, each with its unique animal and pronunciation. Here are some examples from each language family:

Bantu Languages:

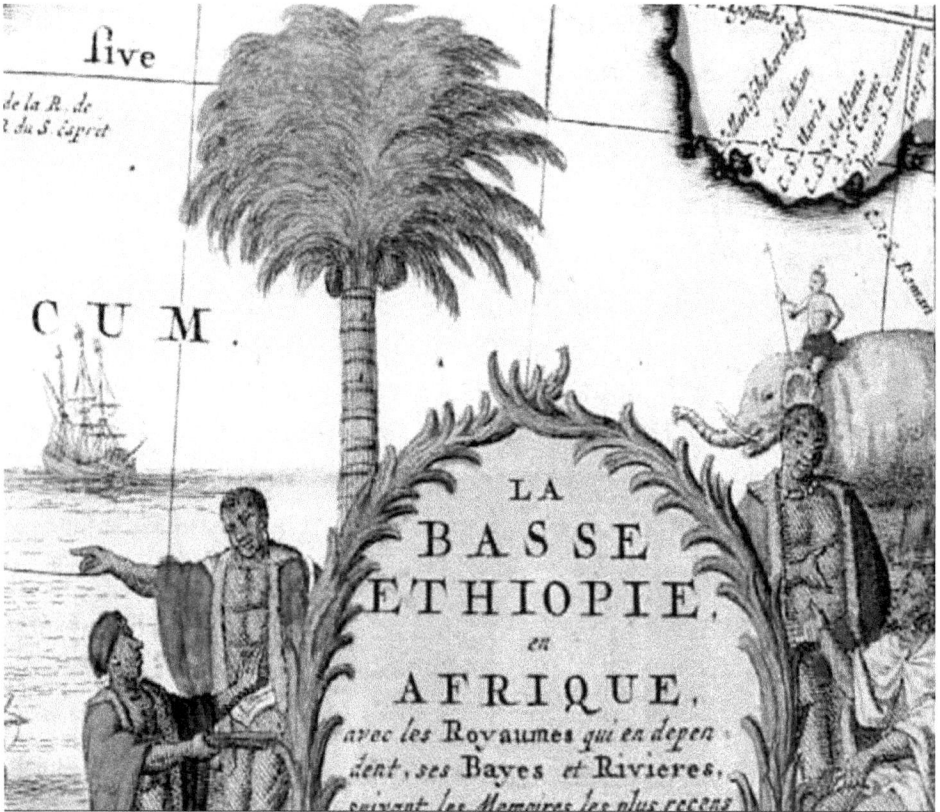

Southern Africa, by Pieter van der Aa. 1713

Swahili: Tembo [pronunciation: tem-bo]
Zulu: Indlovu [pronunciation: een-dlo-voo]
Shona: Nzou [pronunciation: nzoh]
Xhosa: Indlovu [pronunciation: een-dlo-voo]
Kikuyu: Ndovu [pronunciation: ndoh-voo]
Sotho: Tlou [pronunciation: tlo-oo]

Khoisan Languages:
!Xóõ: ǀhàù [pronunciation: ǀhàù]
Nama: !óab [pronunciation: !óab]

There are many more Bantu and Khoisan languages with their own words and pronunciations for "elephant." Pronunciations can vary due to different dialects and regional accents within each language.

The Afroasiatic language family is also quite diverse, and it includes languages spoken across a wide range of countries and

regions. Here are the words for "elephant" in some national Afroasiatic languages.

AFRICAE TABULA

Christoph Weigel (*1654 - †1725)
Old coloured map of the African continent. Printed in Nuremberg
by Johann Ernst Adelbulner in 1718.

Arabic (Standard): فيل (feel)
Hebrew: פיל (peel)
Amharic: ዝሆን (nech)
Hausa: Fílí
Somali: Sandheere
Oromo: Eleefantii
Tigrinya: ዝሆን (nech)
Amazigh/Berber (Tamazight): □□□□□□

Here's the word "elephant" and its pronunciation in various European national languages.

English: Elephant [ˈɛlɪfənt]
French: Éléphant [el-e-fahn]
German: Elefant [ˌeːləˈfant]
Spanish: Elefante [eˈlefante]
Italian: Elefante [eˈlɛfante]
Portuguese: Elefante [ɛlɨˈfẽtɨ]
Dutch: Olifant [ˈoːlɪfɑnt]
Swedish: Elefant [ɛlɛˈfant]
Danish: Elefant [eləˈfɑn]
Norwegian: Elefant [ˈɛləfɑnt]
Finnish: Elefantti [ˈelefɑntːi]
Polish: Słoń [swɔɲ]
Russian: Слон [slon]
Greek: Ελέφαντας [eˈlefandas]
Turkish: Fil [fil]
Czech: Slon [slon]
Hungarian: Elefánt [ɛlɛfaːnt]
Romanian: Elefant [eˈlefant]
Bulgarian: Слон [slon]
Croatian: Slon [slɔ̌ n]

"War elephant" in every Nilo-Saharan and Bantu language, as well as the Khoisan languages,
Nilo-Saharan Languages:
Luo: Nyathi marwe [literally: "war elephant"]

Dinka: Ciib (Ayuel) [literally: "elephant of war"]
Nuer: Ciöc ru [literally: "elephant of war"]
Shilluk: Çöç raññik [literally: "elephant of war"]

Bantu Languages:
Swahili: Tembo wa vita [literally: "elephant of war"]
Zulu: Indlovu yezulu [literally: "elephant of the heavens"]
Shona: Nzou yechimbakadzi [literally: "elephant of war"]
Xhosa: Indlovu yokuthiwa [literally: "elephant of war"]

Khoisan Languages:
!Xóõ: !ná xoa [literally: "fighting elephant"]
Nama: ǀẖùu tso [literally: "war elephant"]
Sure, here's the phrase "elephant rider" in the languages you listed, along with their pronunciations:

The Royal African War Elephant

Afroasiatic Languages:

Arabic: سائق الفيل (sa'iq al-feel) [pronunciation: sah-eek al-feel]
Hebrew: פיל רוכב (rokhav peel) [pronunciation: roh-khav peel]
Amharic: ነጭ መራት (nech marat) [pronunciation: nɛtʃ mar-at]
Hausa: Rana fili [pronunciation: rah-na fee-lee]

Somali: Roobabka sandheere [pronunciation: roh-bahb-ka sahn-dheh-re]

Oromo: Qulqulluu eleefantii [pronunciation: kool-koo-loo el-ee-fan-tee]

Tigrinya: ነጭ ብቅልብ (nech bikilbib) [pronunciation: nɛtʃ be-kee-lee-beeb]

Berber (Tamazight): ⵏⵏⵏⵏⵏⵏⵏ ⵏ ⵏⵏⵏⵏⵏⵏ (axaggan n ilfanṭ) [pronunciation: ah-xahg-gan n il-fahnṭ]

Nilo-Saharan Languages:

Luo: Nyathi modong' [literally: "elephant rider"]
Dinka: Ciib cec [literally: "elephant rider"]
Nuer: Ciöc ca [literally: "elephant rider"]
Shilluk: Çöç ca [literally: "elephant rider"]

Bantu Languages:

Swahili: Mpanda tembo [pronunciation: m-pahn-da tem-bo]
Zulu: Umqhele tembo [pronunciation: oom-khe-le tem-bo]
Shona: Kukwira nzou [pronunciation: koo-kwee-rah nzoh]
Xhosa: Umqhele othwalayo [pronunciation: oom-khe-le oh-thwa-la-yo]

Khoisan Languages:

!Xóõ: ǀxam kū [literally: "elephant rider"]
Nama: ǁî xôa [literally: "elephant rider"]

"The fervent, indomitable spirit of the natural man, and our ancient African civilizations' origins, have always generally been unstoppable by what is undoubtedly divine nature within man. Beginning with the full fervent resistance of incoming back migrations of descendants of Africans to develop their own identities and push back into ancestral lands that were no longer considered their own.

From the ancient, unfortunate annihilation of Neanderthal species and its subgroups, indigenous people lost ground time and time again but always regained it by the course of nature. The Africans who migrated out and mixed with civilizations, such as in Greek invasions Roman invasions, and many others, not only had the full knowledge of their ancestry and kinsmanship of African people but over time, this weighed in on the consciousness of the invaders. It was also due to the sheer understanding of being met with such force and power and the use of war elephants, rhinos, and many different assortments of beasts and large horned cattle, which have long been forgotten by some and have become legends and myths to others.

That same dominating spirit of kingship throughout Kush spread to the West and South, even into the times of the emergence of Islam. These kingdoms fought against slavery, regardless of religion,

banning it. They continued to resist through the modern era in Haitian revolutions and among Africans in America. The great African kings and queens, as well as their descendants from the 18th century to the present, culminated in the independence of African states. This led to the reclamation of national and royal lands on the continent and a re-establishment of societal systems.

Notable figures include:

- **Queen Amanirenas of Kush (Nubia):** She led the Kushite resistance against Roman forces in the 1st century BCE and successfully defeated them.

Jugurthine War
(112-105 BC): The most famous Numidian rebellion was the Jugurthine War, led by Jugurtha, a Numidian noble. Jugurtha's rebellion was fueled by disputes over the Roman client king system and allegations of corruption and bribery in Rome. The war lasted for several years, and it was marked by political intrigue, betrayals, and shifting alliances. Gaius Marius and Lucius Cornelius Sulla, two prominent Roman generals, played roles in the conflict. Eventually, Rome emerged victorious, and Jugurtha was captured.

Zanj Rebellion:
The Zanj Rebellion (869-883) in the Abbasid Caliphate, although not against a European power, was a major slave revolt in the region that resisted Arab rule.

- **Queen Nzinga (Njinga) of Ndongo and Matamba:**
She was a 17th-century queen of the Ndongo and Matamba kingdoms in modern-day Angola and is known for her resistance against Portuguese colonialism.

Ashanti Empire:
Engaged in conflicts with the British, including the Ashanti-British "War of the Golden Stool" (1900), resisting British attempts to control their kingdom.

Zulu Kingdom:
Resisted British colonial expansion during the Anglo-Zulu War (1879).

Algeria:
Fiercely resisted French colonization during the 19th century.

Morocco:
Resisted European colonial ambitions, particularly from France and Spain, throughout the 19th and early 20th centuries.

Maji Maji Rebellion:

Various ethnic groups united to resist German colonial rule in German East Africa (now Tanzania) during the Maji Maji Rebellion (1905-1907).

Samory Touré's Wassoulou Empire:
Led resistance efforts against French expansion in West Africa during the late 19th century.

Mau Mau Uprising:
Significant anti-British rebellion against colonial rule in Kenya during the Mau Mau Uprising (1952-1960).

Ethiopia:
Successfully resisted Italian colonization attempts during the First Italo-Ethiopian War (1895-1896), defeating Italian forces at the Battle of Adwa.

King Shaka Zulu:
He was a 19th-century Zulu king known for his military prowess and efforts to defend Zulu territory against British and Boer forces.

- **Samori Touré:**
A 19th-century leader in West Africa, he resisted French colonial expansion and fought to maintain the sovereignty of the Wassoulou Empire.

In the Americas:

- **Haitian Revolution Leaders:**

Figures like Toussaint Louverture, Jean-Jacques Dessalines, and Henri Christophe led the Haitian Revolution (late 18th to early 19th century) against French colonial rule, resulting in the establishment of Haiti as the first independent Black republic.

- **Harriet Tubman:**

A prominent African American abolitionist who played a significant role in the Underground Railroad, helping enslaved individuals escape to freedom.

Kwame Nkrumah:

He was a key figure in Ghana's struggle for independence from British colonial rule and became the country's first Prime Minister and later its President.

Jomo Kenyatta:

He was a leader in the fight for Kenyan independence from British colonialism and later became the first President of Kenya.

Nelson Mandela:

A prominent anti-apartheid activist who fought against racial segregation in South Africa and became the country's first Black President.

- **Kwame Ture (formerly Stokely Carmichael):**

A leader in the American Civil Rights Movement and a prominent figure in the fight for racial equality in the United States.

These are just a few of the many individuals who have made significant contributions to the fight for freedom, independence, and the preservation of African heritage. Their efforts have had a lasting impact on the history of Africa and the African diaspora."

"Undoubtedly, it is one of the most interesting and ironic occurrences in human history where the people of mixed-race descendants and mixed-race ancestors, born out of the mixed race of a conquering Empire and a subjugated group, embodied both aspects. They became how the conquering group sought to control the oppressed, as well as the mixed-race oppressed who gained the prestige of the conquering Empire. They embodied both identities and eventually became instrumental in the overthrow of the conquering group using their shared identity, uniting people with personal grievances against each other, and seeking retribution for past injustices. Even in ancient times, we see examples of this dynamic. The Hebrew people, an oppressed group within ancient Egypt, known as the land of Khem, eventually emerged from their oppression. They became an African people born out of Egypt by the divine will of God. They were given a distinct identity, becoming a great mixed multitude of people that included not only the oppressed Hebrews but also individuals from all of Egypt. Every one of that day desired to become one nation, and this transformation illustrates the power of shared identity and unity in the face of oppression."

This narrative highlights the historical significance of shared identity and unity in overcoming oppression and seeking justice. The near-conclusion As we embark on the task of chronicling the somber sagas of human strife and the stark inequalities that have etched themselves upon our past, we are faced with an unerring truth - a truth steeped in suffering and agony. Within the very fabric of conflict, a toll is taken, measured not in coin but in the precious essence of existence - the blood of the blameless, the wisdom of the elders, and even the unborn's potential. Amidst this desolation, a different facet emerges, glistening with radiant hope. A tale of fortitude unfurls, revealing the majestic bravery of those who withstand the tempests and rise above the ashes of adversity. This narrative stands as a testament to the resolute spirit inherent to humanity.

It was an interesting thought, to those nations who mastered and tamed the Asian elephants and continued a tradition to do so, where they are now, they are more independent than African nations, and they still use the elephant in society more than just for amusement. Amusement they are part of the customs, part of traditions, and or still a part of military formations to this day. Should not think that what is bending to be a prized weapon of defense throughout the ages is to be deemed irrelevant. Although a countermeasure has shown itself to be formidable is an improper perspective. Even though the elephant gun was coined to mow down the elephant and the cannons for the destruction of the beast as an engine of war, the elephant as a war engine steel holds value to this date and should be

reinstated throughout all African nations as a means of war in a collapse of society and means of transport vehicle productions. Because slaves are not and never have been the source of African wealth and trade. It has always been the might of a king of the jungle, the African war, and the elephant. For a case in point, it is common knowledge that the native Americans are against the expansion of the Europeans lost by way of the attack on the buffalo food source and wildlife Tamed as instruments of war.

Solutions "End Hunting"

"Moreover, it is crucial to emphasize that ending hunting, especially of endangered species like elephants, is a critical component of conservation efforts. In this context, we can deduce with certainty that legal hunting, often referred to as trophy hunting, can have detrimental effects on already vulnerable populations. Henceforth, we can confidently affirm that it can lead to significant population declines, disrupt social structures within animal populations, reduce genetic diversity, and create perverse incentives for poaching.

To elaborate further on this point, we must acknowledge that legal hunting raises ethical concerns and can damage the reputation of countries that permit it. In essence, we can conclude that instead of hunting, alternative conservation approaches, such as community-based conservation and sustainable wildlife tourism, can generate revenue for local communities without relying on hunting.

To reiterate succinctly, it's essential to carefully manage the transition away from hunting and consider the interests of local communities that depend on these activities for their livelihoods. Sustainable alternatives must be developed to ensure that the cessation of hunting does not harm these communities and that conservation efforts are adequately funded and supported.

To put it simply, in light of these considerations, we can assert that ending hunting, particularly of endangered species, is a significant step towards effective conservation."

"While it is easy to suggest measures that could create sustainability, it's important to recognize that there are often costs associated with such initiatives. However, many different methods and approaches can be considered to promote the greater role of elephants in society, fostering human dependency for the survival of ecosystems and species. One significant approach is ecotourism, which can be developed responsibly to provide local communities with economic benefits while promoting the conservation of elephants and their habitats. Concurrently, educational initiatives about elephants and their ecological importance can raise awareness among both local communities and tourists about the value of protecting these magnificent creatures.

Moreover, investing in scientific research to better understand elephant behavior, ecology, and migration patterns is crucial. This knowledge can lead to more informed conservation strategies.

Establishing and maintaining protected areas where elephants can roam freely is another vital step in conserving their natural habitats.

Mitigating conflicts between humans and elephants is paramount. Developing strategies and technologies, such as elephant-proof barriers and early-warning systems, can help minimize such conflicts. Additionally, creating opportunities for local communities to be directly involved in elephant conservation efforts, including training and employment in wildlife monitoring and protection, can foster a sense of shared responsibility.

Promoting sustainable agricultural practices that do not encroach upon elephant habitats and that minimize crop damage by elephants is essential. Exploring non-invasive methods of elephant transportation, such as using elephants for eco-friendly tourism experiences that do not harm the animals, can also play a part.

International cooperation is crucial in combating the illegal wildlife trade and ensuring the protection of elephants across their range of countries. Enforcement and strengthening of laws and policies that protect elephants and their habitats, while discouraging illegal activities such as poaching and habitat destruction, are fundamental steps towards their conservation.

In conclusion, addressing the costs and challenges of sustainability is a complex endeavor, but by employing a multifaceted approach that considers the needs of both elephants and local communities, we can create a sustainable framework. In this framework,

elephants play a vital role in maintaining ecosystems and species survival, while also benefiting human societies."

For those who may question or downplay the importance of this matter and wonder about its relevance to our current circumstances, allow me to clarify. This situation is truly remarkable and carries significant weight, particularly for specific individuals. It deeply resonates with those who possess imaginative minds—those who grasp the profound impact of history, power, and the spiritual essence of life.

It holds a special significance for the up-and-coming creative thinkers who are shaping the narratives that will influence the future of our human race. This is precisely why it holds significance and for whom it holds the utmost importance. It matters to all of us, collectively. Its significance is so substantial that it warrants the construction of monuments across the continent—symbols of historical achievements and sources of inspiration for defenders of ancient military excellence.

We encounter these monuments even in regions where elephants are not native, underscoring their universal relevance. It is not a hidden fact that priceless artifacts and monuments have been lost to destruction, and any that can be salvaged should be, accompanied by reparations. Nevertheless, a more enduring solution lies in the shared memory of future generations and tributes to memorials that will proudly endure for a millennium and beyond.

This monumental approach finds agreement across cultural, religious, and community domains. The understanding is that the outcomes are in the hands of individual communities and organizations dedicated to preserving these historical endeavors. At its core, it is a human issue. The results of war itself always destroy, and from the outset of this literary work, we hope then focus on the lives lost and the countless souls silenced—these are the true losses: time, history, and humanity. This is about us— who we are and how we care for one another—because our stories belong to us. They are our identities. A case in point is Belgium, Leopold in the Belgium colonies of Congo massacred countless souls and The Congo war museum was home to a war elephant statue, one of the only war elephant statues in sub-Saharan Africa, exiting the colonies Belgium took a countless number of Congolese artifacts and materials as well as the more elephant statue that now sits in Belgium that belongs in the Congo to the people of the Congo. At this present time, Congo is requesting the return of the statue while Belgium disputes the need to with trivial responses. So what can be said to this, may need not even be spoken.

But as the banner of victory is unfurled, shadows cast a pall, shrouding the jubilation. The triumphant echoes of one civilization, one tribe, one nation resonate, rippling through the scrolls of history. Yet this triumphant march often carries within it the specter of devastation, the chains of subjugation, the tendrils of deprivation for other people. Amidst the crucible of African history, the intricacies intertwine, unveiling the stark dichotomy of our journey. From the birth pains of nations and peoples emerges a symphony -

a symphony composed of strife and sacrifice, of courage and valor, of lives surrendered and homelands defended. Here, amidst the crucible of trials, courage and mettle weave a splendid tableau, a testament to the undying strength of the human soul.

"And finally
"unequivocally, that great American blockage must be broken. The great Western blockage of the image of African people stumbling afoot and afraid of every African animal must be broken.

Throughout the entire beginning of the 18th century and the rise of Western powers, there has been an agenda to never show the image of an African or Black king or person riding an elephant or rhinoceros in tribal attire, or, should I say, in their national regalia of origin.

It is even difficult to find images of Africans standing next to an elephant in their national tribal regalia or tribal attire. But they do exist, and just the notion that there is a separation between the African and the elephant throughout history is astoundingly ridiculous. When one has a few pieces of history, you learn that elephant hunts produce orphaned calves, automatically creating the opportunity for taming and training. And this is just simple common sense, that people tamed and trained young calves who were orphaned, and the notion that only a few African empires utilized this basic common sense should be a hate crime in itself."

"And it is the African bloodlines, civilizations, and kingdoms that of a prehistoric witch, living with the elephant, rhino, and every animal known to the continent today. Think on this for a moment: it should be suspected that travelers and historians who journeyed to the continent and its kingdoms and did not write about elephants or their interactions with people, other than hunting, ought to automatically raise eyebrows. Because it's human instinct to gravitate towards those fearsome giants of power, to observe how fast they move, as well as how slow, how big they are, and how people naturally interact with them out of curiosity. In general, just seeing the elephant and how people interact with it is reason enough to travel to the continent.

For thousands of years, they have eaten with the elephant, trained with the elephant, sang songs with the elephant, danced with the elephant, and the elephant has known the voices of African people, their tribes, languages, the music of their instruments, the sounds of war, the sounds of children, the sounds of laughter, and even the sounds of horror. All of this should explain the instinctual bond that the people of Africa and Asia had with training these animals. It's at this juncture that it is noted that in the Greek and Roman representations, these animals in war were often mounted by the people who knew them best."

And as we reflect upon the battles waged by the empires of old across the expanse of Africa - the North, the South, the West, and the East - their tales reverberate within these chronicles. In unity, we listen to the cry that echoes through time, the cry of all

descendants of Mother Africa - those who have been lost to the annals of history, to the ravages of war, to the scourge of enslavement, or the dominion of empires. We stand as one, connected by blood, by shared family history, and by unyielding determination

. We pay homage to the valiant warriors and peoples of the continent - those who fought the struggle for self-determination and spiritual enlightenment, seeking the recognition and right to eternal life and generational freedom their voices resonate within us, shaping our collective journey forward. Into the second edition of The Royal African War Elephant, there shall be the travels, the custom, and the artifacts.

In the days when these living souls walked as kings and lived as men, it became evident that they were not only created in the image of God, but they carried within them a divine spark of greatness. Their reigns were not just temporal, but a reflection of a higher design. As we unearth their stories and celebrate their legacies, we recognize that in them, the essence of divinity intertwined with the human experience, leaving an indelible mark on the annals of history. These kings, our brothers, our families, and our histories, embody the enduring connection between the earthly and the divine, reminding us that our journeys are entwined with the eternal.

Special Thanks

I want to express my sincere appreciation to the following individuals and organizations who have played an integral role in the creation of this work:

Director Marquis Burton and the entire team at Urban I Publishing - Your collaborative efforts, mini consultations, and invaluable guidance throughout the publication process have been instrumental in shaping this project. Your vision and expertise have elevated this work to new heights.

To Abdoulie Loveisa Suma, our family in The Gambia, special thanks for the interviews, knowledge, and clarity given.

To Kibri Sulaiman of Nigeria - I extend my gratitude to Kabiru Sulaiman Lawal for the confirmations and consultations. Your involvement has added a unique and meaningful dimension to this project. Olumide, also of Nigeria, deserves special thanks for your contribution and expertise in artwork and graphic design.

Collins Omaghe, my editor, also from Nigeria - for your expertise and creative vision, which have been instrumental in refining and perfecting this manuscript, I want to say thank you.

I also want to thank Lucy Champion for her editorial contributions to the success of this piece of work.

I also want to acknowledge the many others who will assist throughout my upcoming visits to regions and nations across the continent in the endeavor to document the second edition of this work, and I am grateful for their forthcoming contributions. With heartfelt appreciation,

Marquett J. Ivy

"Step into the world of literature on our email and Arthur Page. Discover upcoming literary programs, events, and captivating discussions. Need an author for your event? We've got you covered. Plus, explore our Media Management And Publishing services, led by acclaimed author Marquett J Ivy. Let us bring your literary vision to life. Don't miss out – visit our page today and dive into the magic of words and imagination."

mmpandholdings@gmail.com Resource list

Travelogues and Histories:

-Evliya Çelebi travels. "Ottoman Explorations of the Nile: "
- "The Rihla" by Ibn Battuta
- "The Muqaddimah" by Ibn Khaldun
"Masalik al-Absar fi Mamalik al-Amsar" by Al-Umari
"Kitab al-Masalik wa al-Mamalik" by Al-Bakri
- "Histories" by Herodotus
- "Bibliotheca historica" (Library of History) by Diodorus Siculus
- "African People in World History" by John Henrik Clarke

Additional Authors

- Winters, 2005 -
Hansberry, 1981 - "Pillars in Ethiopian History"
- McAlpin, 1974, 1981 -
- Winters, 1989 -
- Aravanan, 1980 -
- Winters, 2007 -
- Lal, 1963 - "The C-Group People in India and the Origin of Dravidian Speakers"
- Singh, 1982 -
- Aravanan, 1979, 1980 -
- Upadhyaya and Upadhyaya, 1976, 1979 -
- Winters, 1985a, 1988, 1989 -
- Winters, 2000 -

J.A. Rogers' Works
:- "Nature Knows No Color Line: Research into the Negro Ancestry in the White Race"
"100 Amazing Facts About the Negro with Complete Proof: A Short Cut to The World History of The Negro"
"Africa's Gift to America: The Afro-American in the Making and Saving of the United States"
- "World's Great Men of Color" (Vols. 1-2)

"Sex and Race: A History of White, Negro, and Indian Miscegenation in the Two Americas: The New World, 1492-1900"
"Superman to Man"
"From 'Superman' to Man"
"The Five Negro Presidents: According to What White People Said They Were"
- "The Real Facts About Ethiopia"
Dr. Ben's Works:
- "Black Man of the Nile and His Family"
- "We, the Black Jews: Witness to the 'White Jewish Race' Myth, Volumes I &
- "Africa: Mother of Western Civilization"
- "Black Man of the Nile"
"Cultural Genocide in the Black and African Studies Curriculum"

"The Myth of Exodus and Genesis and the Exclusion of Their African Origins"
- "African Origins of the Major Western Religions"
- "The Need for a Black Bible"
"The African Origin of Christianity"- "The African Origin of Freemasonry: African and Moorish Origins of Freemasonry"